TAR HEEL TOWNS, DAY TRIPS
AND WEEKENDS

A FIELD GUIDE TO YOUR NORTH CAROLINA GETAWAY

What to do, where to eat, and how to make
the most of a North Carolina road trip

FROM

Our State
NORTH CAROLINA

GREENSBORO, N.C.

TAR HEEL TOWNS, DAY TRIPS
AND WEEKENDS

A FIELD GUIDE TO YOUR NORTH CAROLINA GETAWAY

What to do, where to eat, and how to make
the most of a North Carolina road trip

Published by *Our State* magazine, Greensboro, N.C.

Tar Heel Towns, Day Trips, and Weekends
copyright © 2011 by *Our State* magazine.
All rights reserved.
Published by Mann Media Inc.
P.O. Box 4552, Greensboro, N.C. 27404
(800) 948-1409; www.ourstate.com
Printed in the United States by R.R. Donnelley

Editor: Elizabeth Hudson
Art Director: Deanne O'Connor
Editorial Intern: Chantel O'Neal

Library of Congress Control Number:
2011927881

TAR HEEL TOWNS, DAY TRIPS
AND WEEKENDS
A FIELD GUIDE TO YOUR NORTH CAROLINA GETAWAY

TABLE OF CONTENTS

Asheboro

Blowing Rock

Kill Devil Hills

From the center of Hot Springs, take the Lover's Leap Hike, an hour-long walk that will take you to this vantage point, where you can view the town and mountains in the distance.

HOT SPRINGS

Ron West grabs the hammer from the backseat of his Chevy pickup before getting out. As he approaches a raised manhole oddly placed in the middle of the woods, he draws his hammer back, swings, and locks its claws underneath the manhole's handle on his first try. Slowly, he lifts the iron lid, and a mixture of steam and warmth kisses the fresh air. Inside the hole, pipes rise up from a pool of crystal clear water that's about six feet deep. "Our hottest spring comes out of the ground at 108 degrees," he explains. West brags about this natural phenomenon like a proud father. The manhole, as it turns out, covers a hot hole where mineral water is pumped from natural hot springs — the only hot springs known to be in North Carolina.

MAGIC WATERS

For centuries, the waters of Hot Springs and their "healing powers" have lured folks to this tiny community in western Madison County. West and his wife, Sandy, have lived in Hot Springs since 1979, and they manage Hot Springs Resort and Spa. The Wests say the town was a ghost town before the springs reopened in 1990. "It really opened up Hot Springs again," Ron says. The key word in that sentence is again. Although this small town doesn't have any stoplights, Hot Springs has a rather glamorous past.

Surrounded by the Blue Ridge Mountains, the Pisgah National Forest, and the French Broad River, Hot Springs' terrain has always been pristine. The Appalachian Trail runs straight through town, further proving that you're in the midst of a Sierra Club dream. Such a place is fitting for a resort destination. Add the mystical waters that come up from the ground and have been known to ease physical ailments, and you've got a natural paradise.

Believed to be used first by the Cherokee Indians, the springs were discovered by white settlers in 1778. Thirteen years later, William Nelson bought the hot springs property, and the town's foray into tourism began. Initially named Warm Springs, the town got a boost in 1827 when the Buncombe Turnpike was completed. A couple of hotels followed, as the town earned an international reputation for its magical waters. The Warm Springs Hotel had a dining room that could seat 600 before it burned in 1884. The Mountain Park Hotel, complete with four stories, more than 1,000 feet of piazzas, and a bathhouse with 16 marble-lined pools,

During a snowfall, he saw a spot in the woods where the snow was melted. Sure enough, he discovered the location of the hot spring.

was built in 1886 — the same year a hotter spring was discovered, spurring the town's name change to Hot Springs. During the early 20th century, when World War I hijacked everyone's attention, business slowed, and the hotel served as an internment camp for German merchant sailors. The hotel burned in 1920.

Hot Springs became even more isolated when Interstate 40 was built south of town in the 1960s. Visitors became few and far between.

However, one visitor who stopped by in 1956 turned out to be a rescuer of sorts. Eugene Hicks, a Madison County native, was home from the military when he stopped by The Hot Springs Inn to ask if he could look around. "They told him, 'No, registered guests only. Be on your way,'" Sandy West explains. The refusal upset Hicks so much that he vowed he would one day buy the 100-acre property, and that's exactly what he did 34 years later.

Hicks lived in a camper-trailer as he tried to clear the neglected property and find out where the springs were. During a snowfall, he saw a spot in the woods where the snow was melted. Sure enough, he discovered the location of the hot spring. Instead of renovating the bathhouse and its marble tubs, which still stand on the property today, he decided to pump the water into modern hot tubs. And he waited for people to come.

People did come, and lots of people come now, including such celebrities as Lance Armstrong, Robert Redford, and the Dalai Lama. While the guest list includes the rich and famous, Hot Springs is hardly exclusive. Because of how Hicks was treated on that day in 1956, he was adamant that Hot Springs Resort and Spa be a working-person's spa — a spa that the average working family could afford to enjoy.

— *Lori Tate*

While you're here: After relaxing in the springs, visit the shops at The Iron Horse Station (opposite, top left); then take a stroll down to Gentry Hardware, where Keith Gentry and his fiancée, Jeanne Caldwell, continue the family business that started right after World War II.

HOW TO EXPERIENCE HOT SPRINGS:

1. Get wet! You are here for the springs, after all.

Hot Springs Resort and Spa
315 Bridge Street
Hot Springs, N.C. 28743
(828) 622-7676

2. Pick up a hiking map or a sleeping-bag liner at **Bluff Mountain Outfitters**, the go-to place for rafters and hikers on the Appalachian Trail to restock their packs.

Bluff Mountain Outfitters
152 Bridge Street
Hot Springs, N.C. 28743
(828) 622-7162

3. Eat a MoonPie dipped in dark chocolate at **Tootsie's Apple Basket** on Willy's Corner, where Tootsie Gregory sells homemade goodies.

Tootsie's Apple Basket
123 North Spring Street
Hot Springs, N.C. 28743
(828) 206-4178

4. Spend a few hours inside The Iron Horse Station, a beautifully restored group of historic buildings that includes a restaurant, tavern, inn, and shop filled with the work of local artists.

The Iron Horse Station
24 South Andrews Avenue
Hot Springs, N.C. 28743
(828) 622-0022

5. Order The Skillet Breakfast — chunked potatoes with meat and green peppers, onions, and mushrooms, all smothered in cheese and served in an iron skillet with the eggs on top — at the **Smoky Mountain Diner.** The diner is open 365 days a year and even serves a traditional Christmas dinner complete with turkey, ham, sweet potato casserole, and red velvet cake.

Smoky Mountain Diner
70 Lance Avenue
Hot Springs, N.C. 28743
(828) 622-7571

Viewed from the High Hampton Inn and Country Club, sunrise is an experience in Cashiers.

CASHIERS

In a far southwestern corner of North Carolina, in a village that sits 3,486 feet above anything along the coast, you first grasp the local love affair with nature at the intersection of N.C. Highway 107 and U.S. Highway 64, the village center known as the "Crossroads."

There's a gas station, a coffee shop, and a farmers market with peaches, sunflowers, strawberry-rhubarb spread, and a potbellied pig named B.B. And catty-corner from the coffee shop called Buck's, behind a low stone wall, you discover a big playground, winding paths, and a sculpture garden with this statement: "It is here where we rest and dream."

Rest here near sunset, on that low stone wall, and you'll catch the slight smell of honeysuckle, the playful screams of a little girl, and the sight of two couples walking by, must be in their 80s. They're hand in hand. They meander down a path, past two sculptures of big snails, into a park.

This all happens in minutes at dusk in the Village Green, the heart of a place called Cashiers.

A SPECIAL PLACE

Like many towns in North Carolina, Cashiers has a pronunciation all its own.

It's called CASH-urs. It has nothing to do with money; the name comes from a mispronunciation of one of Wade Hampton's bulls.

The Civil War general from South Carolina started vacationing here more than a century ago. Today, his former hunting lodge has been turned into an inn — the High Hampton Inn — with 116 rooms and 17 guest cottages. The rooms have no phone, no TV, no air-conditioning. Meanwhile, there is a rustic Southern gentility — in the dining room, for example, men and boys older than 11 are required to wear a coat and tie — that you won't find hardly anywhere else. And

there's a world-famous golf course, legendary fried chicken, a garden of century-old dahlias, and an old-fashioned feel.

THE ROOTS OF BEAUTY

In Cashiers, nature is the main event. Sit at the base of Silver Run Falls, just south of the High Hampton, and you'll be inside a coliseum of hardwoods and pines, surrounded by the constant swoosh of water. Nothing else.

Stand at the famous No. 8 — the hole at High Hampton that *Golf Digest* calls "one of America's greatest" — and watch the sun rise over Rock Mountain.

Pore through local Cherokee folklore, and you'll read about an immense bird named Tlanuwa that carried off dogs and small children, and a Cherokee witch known as Spearfinger who danced amid the clouds, brandishing a stone forefinger that could kill anyone with the slightest touch.

Both lived in Whiteside Mountain, home of the peregrine falcon and the highest sheer cliff in the eastern United States.

The High Hampton Inn is a world-class getaway in the mountains.

Stand at famous No. 8 — the hole at High Hampton that *Golf Digest* calls "one of America's greatest" — and watch the sun rise over Rock Mountain.

IN SEARCH OF MOUNTAIN TIME

Between April and October, Cashiers swells from 233 people to a population of 25,000. The allure is lengthy: cool summers, breathtaking autumns, 60 miles of golf fairways, and those serendipitous moments in and around the Village Green.

Locals and visitors protect this allure with missionary zeal, and the reason is simply in the numbers: at least 10 hiking trails, 11 waterfalls, and 15 fly-fishing streams, full of trout. Mountains are everywhere you look.

The trails, waterfalls, and mountain scenery are all within minutes of the "Crossroads," a place where you can drink good coffee, read a book, and hear someone explain his idea of mountain time: You get there when you get there; you get it done when you get it done. — *Jeri Rowe*

HOW TO EXPERIENCE CASHIERS:

1. Learn the history. In the 1830s, the Zachary family settled in Cashiers, carving out a living along the Cherokee trails, bartering for eggs, and having their children taught in one-room schoolhouses. In 1842, one of the Zachary sons, Mordecai, began building a house, completed it 10 years later, and presented it to his bride, Elvira. Today, the house is Cashiers' premier historic site.

Zachary-Tolbert House Museum
1940 N.C. Highway 107 South
Cashiers, N.C. 28717
(828) 743-7710
cashiershistoricalsociety.com

2. Eat like a local. Enjoy the farmhouse ambience at **The Orchard**, where local trout and Anson Mill cheese grits are a can't-miss menu staples.

The Orchard Restaurant
905 N.C. Highway 107 South
Cashiers N.C. 28717
(828) 743-7614

3. Wind down on mountain time. Sink into a leather sofa. Drink coffee. Be still.

Buck's Coffee Cafe of Cashiers
6 N.C. Highway 107 North
Cashiers, N.C. 28717
(828) 743-9997

4. Relax, Wade's way. In the 19th century, South Carolina's Gen. Wade Hampton built a hunting lodge in the mountains to escape the oppressive summertime heat. After enduring the Civil War, including the Battle of Gettysburg in 1863, Hampton made his way back to his estate to rest and regain his strength. Listed on the National Register of Historic Places, the estate is still drawing people to its restorative grounds.

The High Hampton Inn
1525 N.C. Highway 107 South
Cashiers, N.C. 28717
(828) 743-2411
highhamptoninn.com

Chad (opposite top, on left) and Travis Boswell (on right) renovated an old house and turned it into The Orchard restaurant.
At the High Hampton Inn, visitors will find loads of Southern charm and even a pair of donkeys — Ed and Fred — and their keeper, James Connor (opposite bottom).
Below: Silver Run Falls is a place to get lost in the sounds of washing water.

Visitors are welcome to attend services at Rumple Memorial Presbyterian Church on Main Street.

3 BLOWING ROCK

On weekdays, town workers let themselves into Tim Knight's restaurant, Knight's On Main, at 5 a.m., in a tradition that started 30 years ago. Tim often arrives at work to find coffee and conversation already brewing.

Sure, this community use of a private business is a bit unorthodox, but Blowing Rock is a town where almost every year-round resident holds a key to someone else's business or home — even the mayor is caretaker to a house not his own.

Ginny Stevens — a sprightly attendant at the tiny white cottage-turned-history-museum adjacent to the town's picturesque Memorial Park — says Blowing Rock's status as a tourist mecca began in the 1800s. When the demand for accommodations grew, the town's grand hotels — The Watauga Hotel, Mayview Manor, and Green Park Inn — were built. Only the Green Park Inn survives, and just barely. The Victorian-era structure was recently purchased by Irace Realty Associates, who are renovating it.

The loss of these early hotels still distresses many people in a town that prides itself on valuing preservation and the arts. These interests are clearly illustrated in the Blowing Rock Art and History Museum, a 21,000-square-foot structure that will house a collection of work by Elliott Daingerfield, a renowned painter and former seasonal resident. The museum, slated to open in fall 2011, and such resources as the Mariam and Robert Hayes Performing Arts Center and even the local hospital are rare for a town the size of Blowing Rock. But tourism and seasonal residents make such luxuries possible.

Blowing Rock has a full-time population of approximately 1,500, but in the summer, the number swells to around 8,000.

The town, founded in 1889, covers three square miles, but its unique, vacation-minded demographic supports more than 100 shops, two-dozen restaurants, and nearly 20 accommodation choices. Up until the 1990s, Blowing Rock boarded up in the winter months, but it has since come into its own as a year-round community, welcoming visitors in all sorts of weather.

FEW SECRETS LEFT

High noon means big traffic at Knight's On Main. It's a weekday, but the gathering crowd doesn't seem to be in a hurry. Knight's On Main is a family restaurant, and if

"They used to sell a tourist book, *Blowing Rock's Best Kept Secrets*. You'd buy it and open it up, and there was nothing in it. There are no secrets in Blowing Rock."

you're a local, you're family.

"It's the sort of place, Blowing Rock, where the police chief still gets out every day and directs school traffic. I know. It's too cute," says Tracy Brown, executive director of the Blowing Rock Tourism Development Authority. "The town is so small they used to sell a tourist book, *Blowing Rock's Best Kept Secrets*. It was wrapped in cellophane. You'd buy it and open it up, and there was nothing in it." He gives a measured pause before delivering the punch line: "There are no secrets in Blowing Rock."

Well, there might be a few. There's Village Café, a lovely restaurant with garden dining that's hidden behind Main Street. And there's Lover's Leap, a lookout in the Mayview neighborhood, former site of Mayview Manor. The landmark is a small clearing at the end of the road, crowned by a rock formation. The outcropping is not as impressive as The Blowing Rock — the storied lookout that gave the town its name — but this beloved spot has a few legends of its own.

In most towns, residents use buildings as landmarks, but in Blowing Rock, nature is the compass.

Knight's On Main specializes in old-fashioned, country cooking.

FROM TOWN TO WILDERNESS

The Glen Burney trail starts roughly a block from Blowing Rock's Main Street. The trailhead is hidden near the Annie L. Cannon Memorial Gardens, behind the parking lot that hosts the popular Art in the Park events from May to October. The trail was formed by Native American hunters and adopted by loggers before becoming the domain of tourists. Today, the steep, 1.5-mile foot trail is a little-known getaway that connects the town to the tip of the Pisgah National Forest.

Tim Gregg knows the trail better than most. He grew up here and was a caretaker of the trail for 15 years, "If you didn't stop by the Visitor Center and nobody told you this was here, you'd never find it," Gregg says. He points to nearby trees and identifies a dizzying variety of species, including witch hazel and red oak.

"I couldn't tell you how many times I've walked this," he says. "Instantly, you go from town to wilderness. I've always loved it."

The trail dead-ends at a 70-foot waterfall that zigzags down, flowing into pools as clear as air.

Suddenly, Gregg stops. There's a crack in the stone. A small fern has found unlikely footing, shooting forth with graceful curves and a formidable life force.

Gregg bends down, shaking his head at the plant's unexpected loveliness. Instinctually, he brings it to the attention of a fellow hiker, eager to share the fragile beauty of his hometown with a guest who's just passing through.

— *Leigh Ann Henion*

HOW TO EXPERIENCE BLOWING ROCK:

1. Take in the view. It's only a short, scenic stroll to see the town's namesake lookout and majestic views of Grandfather Mountain.

Blowing Rock Attraction
432 Rock Road
Blowing Rock, N.C. 28605
(828) 295-7111

2. Explore nature and hike the 1.5-mile Glen Burney trail to catch a glimpse of waterfalls and woodland critters.

Glen Burney Trail & Annie Cannon Memorial Gardens
229 Laurel Lane
Blowing Rock, N.C. 28605
(828) 295-7851

3. Dine on down-home cooking at **Knight's On Main**. Try the famous barbecue ribs — the secret sauce is sold by the jar.

Knight's On Main
870 Main Street
Blowing Rock, N.C. 28605
(828) 295-3869

4. Hop aboard a Wild West train ride at **Tweetsie Railroad**, complete with historic locomotives, cowboys, and train robbers.

Tweetsie Railroad
300 Tweetsie Railroad Lane
Blowing Rock, N.C. 28605
(828) 264-9061

5. Peruse local art at **Main Street Gallery** (across from the post office), where you'll find local-made pottery, jewelry, photography, woodworking, paintings, and more.

Main Street Gallery
960 Main Street
Blowing Rock, N.C. 28605
(828) 295-7839

Dominique Huneycutt and her dog, Mystic, enjoy a day on Main Street.

WEAVERVILLE

WESTERN N.C. | 9 miles north of Asheville | **WEAVERVILLENC.ORG**

Just outside the door of Mangum Pottery, Minnie — a mutt with strong hound-dog leanings — lies curled in a patch of sun. Ankles pass by, inches from her face. Not exactly a sentry, she barely lifts her head to sniff the air.

Inside, owners Rob and Beth Mangum are hard at work. Rob is shaping slabs of clay into the rough form of a three-tiered fountain; Beth is bringing life to the beginnings of a pitcher. An employee, Casey Dougan, stands at a nearby table, packing orders to ship. Tom Waits's voice growls from a speaker above.

The Mangums arrived in this mountain town in 1998 and have been a steady presence ever since. Rob grew up north of Boone, in Ashe County, Beth in northern Virginia. The two met at North Carolina State University's College of Design, did the festival circuit for several years, and by the late 1990s, started looking for a place to put down roots.

A decade later, the five-block stretch of Main Street is home to a half-dozen cafes and restaurants, a fly-fishing outfitter, a renovator's supply company, a spa, and a handful of craft galleries. A yoga studio sits just off the street. The old guard is still in evidence, too: the upholstery shop, the insurance agency, the car-repair shop with bluegrass music spilling from its bays. Compared to the carnival atmosphere of nearby Asheville, Weaverville's compact downtown and quiet cross-streets — lined with dogwoods, redbuds, and bungalows — can seem, well, positively quaint.

BUILT ON DRY GROUND

Weaverville saw its beginnings more than two centuries ago in 1786 when John and Elizabeth Weaver and their son, Jacob, made the trek across the mountains from eastern Tennessee, settling about a quarter-mile east of where downtown rises today. The area was once known as Dry Ridge for the fact that rainfall was spotty compared to the surrounding mountains. That distinction survives today in the names of a number of local businesses: Dry Ridge Inn, Dry Ridge Family Medicine, and the aptly named Dry Ridge Roofing company.

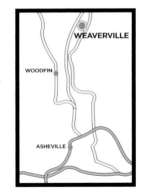

The town followed the classic arc of development, from agriculture to milling, timbering to textiles. By the last years of the 19th century, Weaverville was approaching its commercial zenith, home to grand hotels and places where artists, writers, and captains

Weaverville's compact downtown and quiet cross-streets — lined with dogwoods, redbuds, and bungalows — can seem positively quaint.

of industry came to recover from the dissipations of urban life. A trolley line, spurring north from Asheville, carried passengers to Main Street for the sum of 35 cents.

UP, DOWN, AND BACK

Today, Main Street may not represent the town's commercial center, a distinction that belongs to the strip malls and a handful of new big-box stores just to the west. But it may represent the town's best impulses, a location where newfangled creativity and wireless-enabled coffee shops sit comfortably alongside more traditional enterprises. The former Bank of Weaverville — vault intact — was recently fashioned into an

Aveda salon and spa. And the old drug store is now the Well-Bred Bakery & Cafe. Need a prescription for whatever ails you? A cup of coffee, supplied from Durham's renowned Counter Culture Coffee, and a slice of chocolate fudge cake might do the trick.

Several years ago, the old Baptist church became the local public library branch.

Throughout town, the repurposing of Weaverville's historic buildings continues. Developer Lou Accornero stands outside what was, until recently, the town's fire department. A tape measure clatters against his pant leg as he points out favorite details of the structure: "You see those capitals? They're almost Deco. Beautiful." Downstairs, he places a hand against a wall reverentially. "They tell me that behind this plaster are the old hitches where they tied the horses that pulled the fire wagons. I haven't seen them yet, but they're gonna stay."

— *Kent Priestley*

On Main Street, get your hands on the homemade wares from Mangum Pottery (opposite, top left).

At Well-Bred Bakery & Cafe, Carrie, an English Shepherd, waits patiently beneath a table. Inside, the Strawberry Peanut Butter Cheesecake (opposite, bottom left), takes the cake.

HOW TO HAVE THE WEAVERVILLE EXPERIENCE:

1. Take home a handmade souvenir such as a piece of pottery from the **Mangum Pottery** gallery or a custom-made necklace from **Miya Gallery** next door.

Mangum Pottery
16 North Main Street
Weaverville, N.C. 28787
(828) 645-4929
mangumpottery.com

Miya Gallery
20 North Main Street
Weaverville, N.C. 28787
(828) 658-9655
miyagallery.com

2. Need a new fly reel to experience the area's extraordinary flyfishing? Stop in to **Curtis Wright Outfitters**, and the staff will hook you up.

Curtis Wright Outfitters
24 North Main Street
Weaverville, N.C. 28787
(828) 645-8700
curtiswrightoutfitters.com

3. Come for the menu — hearty eaters will devour the Mountain Extravaganza pizza, loaded with ham, beef, sausage, pepperoni, onions, and a lot more — but stay for the music. Live music adds to the lively atmosphere.

Blue Mountain Pizza
55 North Main Street
Weaverville, N.C. 28787
(828) 658-8777

4. Venture into Shope's Furniture, one of the oldest businesses in town. The upstairs is full of contemporary furnishings, but the downstairs, out of sight, is another world. It was the former town hall and jail, and it still has its old Otis elevator and the old jail's holding cell is down there, too.

Shope's Furniture
31 North Main Street
Weaverville, N.C. 28787
(828) 645-3091

5 BOONE

WESTERN N.C. | 8 miles north of Blowing Rock | **VISITBOONENC.COM**

What are those? Paper lanterns, beehives? Scotty Prevost, store manager at Boone Drug Fountain and Grill, hears all kinds of guesses about the yellowing prescription papers that hang, stacked like pancakes, on coat hangers. Ironically, the flagship store, now half soda fountain-half sundry, no longer fills prescriptions. Before 8 a.m. every weekday, the grill sizzles as workers fry eggs and sausage for regulars, or Coffee Club members, who arrive one by one, as they have for generations.

Former town mayor Wade Wilmoth has shown up at Boone Drug faithfully each morning since the 1970s, where he says he learned more about what was going on in town than in his board meetings. "There's something about Boone," he says. "I've traveled all over the state, and no matter where I go, people know about it ... Just mentioning it makes people smile. Boone's magic."

The Coffee Club spirals down to a favorite discussion — bemoaning the parking situation. At this, Wilmoth puts up a hand. "The worst problem a town can have is no parking problem," he says. Boone is a town of 15,000, not counting tourists and Appalachian State University students — and everyone seems to crave time downtown.

It's getting late in the morning when Wilmoth spots a table of people he doesn't recognize. He can't contain his curiosity and leans in. "Excuse me. Where are you from?" One woman replies, "Fort Mill, South Carolina."

Wilmoth smiles. "Well, welcome to Boone. We're glad to have you!" Just like that, the Coffee Club temporarily gains a few extra members.

BOONERANG'

Boone is a difficult town to leave. For years, that was more literal, due to two-lane mountain roads. But even with the widening of highways, it's still true in an emotional sense. Locals call it: Boonerang. If you leave, you're probably going

College students and tourists alike keep King Street in downtown Boone humming with activity year-round.

HOW TO EXPERIENCE BOONE:

1. Join the regulars for a country-style breakfast at **Boone Drug Fountain and Grill**, serving the town for 92 years and counting.

Boone Drug Fountain and Grill
617 West King Street
Boone, N.C. 28607
(828) 264-3766

2. Catch a show at **Horn in the West**, where outdoor Revolutionary War dramas have portrayed the life of Blue Ridge Mountain settlers since 1952.

Horn in the West
591 Horn in the West Drive
Boone, N.C. 28607
(828) 264-2120

3. String a necklace and matching earrings from the array of semiprecious stones, wild amulets, and blown-glass charms that fill **The BeadBox**. Don't forget to grab a cup of **Grateful Grounds** coffee to go.

The BeadBox — Grateful Grounds
585 West King Street
Boone, N.C. 28607
(828) 265-2315

4. Strike for gold or more than 40 other minerals at **Foggy Mountain Gem Mine**. Sift through a bucket of ore to find take-home treasures, such as emeralds, amethyst, smoky quartz, and more.

Foggy Mountain Gem Mine
4416 N.C. Hwy 105 South
Boone, N.C. 28607
(828) 963-4367

to come back or, at least, you'll long to.

Ged Moody, director of sustainability at ASU, hasn't been through a Boonerang cycle himself. He moved here to attend graduate school, but when it was time to leave, he couldn't bear the thought. This is another pattern in the picturesque mountain town: ASU graduates many students, but a good number stay.

When Moody tells neighbors what he does for a living, they bring up the wind turbine. Erected in 2009, the 153-foot-tall machine stands watch over Boone — which, at 3,300 feet, is the highest town of its size east of the Mississippi. The turbine, the largest of its kind in the state, came to be because of ASU's Renewable Energy Initiative. "It's not here to make money. It's not here to solve ASU's or Boone's energy needs," Moody says. "It's to help our students learn."

Boone, incorporated in 1872, was named after pioneer Daniel Boone, who supposedly camped near what is now the ASU Duck Pond. The town has long attracted adventurers willing to explore the unknown — and much of modern exploration takes place in the form of research.

A WALKING TOWN

Officer Mike Foley, Boone's downtown beat cop, walks about five miles a day on patrol. In the span of an hour, he's everywhere — downtown alleyways, secret passageways between buildings. And he knows things. He knows where a leaky pipe led to historic photos being lost. Or where, in his opinion, you can find the best chili (Trolly Stop) and who fills his ever-present coffee mug with premium java (The BeadBox). The BeadBox, a make-your-own jewelry store, is also home to the coffee shop Grateful Grounds. The owner, Nikki Burris, moved here from Chicago. When she called her cousin to tell her where she was headed, she heard a gasp: "She said, 'Nikki! Boone is my husband's nickname for me!'" It turns out, her cousin married a road biker who had, for years, been told that Boone was the best place in the country to bike. Boone has quite a reputation among road bikers, partly because of seven-time Tour de France winner Lance Armstrong's affinity for the town.

Foley prefers to walk because, as he says, walking leads to talking. "It's kind of a big family downtown," he says. "People walk rather than drive." So, when in Boone, do as the Boonians do: Find a place to park, and use your own, sustainable locomotion. Before long, you'll find yourself in the middle of a good, old-fashioned conversation in this thoroughly contemporary town. — *Leigh Ann Henion*

Delicious aromas from the cinnamon rolls at Macado's (below, top left) waft down King Street. Officer Mike Foley (below, right) knows the smells well — he walks five miles a day on patrol. Just a few blocks from downtown, at Appalachian State University, football fanatics support their home team.

6 NANTAHALA OUTDOOR CENTER

WESTERN N.C. | 30 miles southwest of Maggie Valley | **NOC.COM**

By the early 1990s, the Nantahala Outdoor Center had begun to grow up — and fast. "During the late 1980s, interest in rafting really took off," explains Lee Leibfarth, NOC's current chief operating officer. "So the business went from being this little niche along the Appalachian Trail to becoming the largest whitewater rafting company in the country." The company has since expanded into a kind of outdoor adventure empire, with satellite locations on the Pigeon, Nolichucky, Chattooga, Ocoee, French Broad, and Cheoah rivers.

The whitewater industry has grown up around Nantahala Outdoor Center, making it just one of 20 rafting companies lining this stretch of river today. But despite the competition, NOC manages to escort more than 80,000 rafters down the river each year, a good number of them residents of regional centers, such as Atlanta, Georgia, and Nashville, Tennessee, freed from their corporate warrens for a weekend of dampish adventure. More recently, NOC has expanded offerings to include fly-fishing, guided hikes, wilderness first-responder training, and international adventure travel, as well as canoeing and kayaking. But in the final score, appetites may trump even adventure here.

AFTER THE RIVER, TRY THE RESTAURANT

A few years ago, we realized that we serve more people at our restaurants than we take down the river," Leibfarth admits. "That was eye-opening." River's End, a restaurant perched along the south bank of the Nantahala River, 12 miles west of Bryson City, offers a perfect lunch for the adventure enthusiast.

The restaurant was founded in 1972, when husband and wife Payson and Aurelia Kennedy and their business partner, Horace Holden Sr., purchased the property that would become the Nantahala Outdoor Center. Back then, the restaurant was a granola-and-herbal-tea affair, a place where mayflies batted against the screens on warm winter days and the waitstaff occasionally had more hair than expertise. The menu, too, reflected a pointedly grassroots approach: Locally harvested watercress, dandelions, and ramps sometimes graced entrees, and daily menus included line drawings of local landmarks and personalities on their covers.

Founder Aurelia Kennedy, who served as River's End's first manager, once sponsored a mail-in contest in which people could send their favorite recipes to the restaurant for use, if worthy, on the menu. In 1983, some

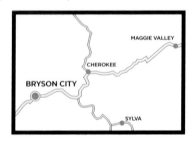

"So the business went from being this little niche along the Appalachian Trail to becoming the largest whitewater rafting company in the country."

of those, and many others, were gathered together and published as *The River Runner's Cookbook*. Now out of print, the book offered wholesome, filling meals that would suit the nutritional needs of trail builders, A.T. hikers, canoeists, fishermen, and generally rugged people. There was the Sherpa, a medley of rice, beans, lentils, cheese, and stir-fried vegetables that the Kennedys concocted while trekking in the Himalayan foothills. An assortment of Sherpa chilis are on the menu today, and are a perfect way to renourish after an invigorating run down the river.

— *Kent Priestley*

Above: Payson and Aurelia Kennedy chose adventure over convention 37 years ago and built a thriving business. Opposite: River's End is one of several quick-serve dining options along the river at NOC.

HOW TO EXPERIENCE THE NOC:

1. Pedal. From rugged mountain biking to road cycling, the NOC offers gear for every rider.

2. Paddle. Kayak across the calm waters of Fontana Lake, or make a splash whitewater rafting down miles of class II and III rapids.

3. Shoot. Bring your camera and capture scenes of the Nantahala National Forest with an Adventure Photography Workshop. Tip: Sign up online before you go.

4. Climb. Tackle the Alpine Tower, a 50-foot-tall structure that's half climbing wall and half jungle gym. Hop across the Floating Logs, and maneuver through the Diabolical See-Saw to reach the top.

5. Refuel. After a long, adventurous day, pull up a riverside seat at one of the four restaurants located right on the property: **River's End, Relia's Garden, Slow Joe's Riverside Cafe,** or **The Pourover,** a favorite for its local beer and live music.

Nantahala Outdoor Center
13077 Highway 19 West
Bryson City, N.C. 28713
(800) 232-7238

6. Ride. Kick back on the **Great Smoky Mountains Railroad,** and chug along the old Murphy Line. Enjoy the view of quaint mountain towns and sparkling rivers from your window.

Great Smoky Mountains Railroad
226 Everett Street
Bryson City, NC 28713
(800) 872-4681
gsmr.com

THE SWAG

A bove Haywood County, where a road with 56 curves will take you 5,000 feet above Jonathan Creek Valley, you'll hear a constant phrase around the scarlet begonias in the roll-away cart: "Oh, that's so Swaggy!"

Being Swaggy — or to be a "Swagger" — is this: Hike six hours, see a bear, play with Malcolm the cat, chuck a horseshoe, or eat fresh mountain trout beneath an antler chandelier that's as big as a bay window. You're surrounded by the smell of the wood, as fresh as morning rain. And you eat food, farm-to-table, garden-fresh food.

And you'll work it off. You'll hike to some place like Boogerman Trail and talk about the bale of wild turkeys you saw. Or you'll crawl from your covers just before daybreak, grab your walking stick, and feel your heartbeat in your neck by the time you reach Gooseberry Knob.

There, you'll see a sunrise that'll feather the clouds with enough colors to exhaust any crayon box. You'll see the stars blink, hear the crackle of a nearby creek, and see mountains rolling toward the horizon. Then, you get it.

'NORTH AMERICAN SHANGRI-LA'

Since 1982, guests have struggled for words to describe this place. You see it in the room journals and thank-you notes. They call it "a sanctuary," "a North American Shangri-la," "my place of peace."

Travelers come from all over the world, to this dip between two mountains known simply as a swag. They come to a country inn, a place of notched logs and big fireplaces that's open between April and November every year and has won acclaim from almost every travel magazine in the world. It sits on 250 acres, within a dozen steps from the Great Smoky Mountains National Park. It's a hiker's resort, with 15 spots to stay with such names as Woodshed, Two-Story, or Danny's Room.

Dan and Deener Matthews bought the property in 1969 to make it a second home that they later turned into a church retreat. But in 1982, it became an inn — by accident.

That summer, the World's Fair came to Knoxville, Tennessee. Hotel rooms close to the event were packed. So, the Matthewses opened up to fairgoers.

Well, those fairgoers never went to

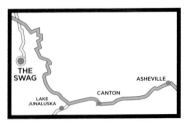

Built with logs purchased from a Primitive Baptist church in Tennessee, The Swag's rustic exterior belies the luxury hidden within.

It's so foggy it looks like an ocean, and the sky is just so red it looks like a dreamland.'

Knoxville. They stayed and fell in love with what they saw. Meanwhile, as she made casseroles for her guests, Deener realized she had a knack for hospitality.

Chef Bryan Kimmett creates his menus from what he buys from local farms, finds at the nearby farmers market in Asheville, or what he plucks from his garden out back. He's from Maryland, a kid who started in the restaurant business at age 15 washing dishes. Now, at 48, he's making pan-roasted quail, pistachio-crusted king salmon, and smoked trout, in crayfish-and-chive oil.

Next, follow gardener Mike Patterson. He'll point out a serviceberry tree, with a trunk as thick as a young man's waist, and dissect the micro-climate in the Smokies, a spot where plants are as diverse as the Amazon.

The Swag
2300 Swag Road
Waynesville, N.C. 28785
(800) 789-7672

Or simply watch Linda Duckett, the pastry chef. She calls herself an old country girl. She came with no confidence. Now, in her third season at The Swag, after taking a few pastry and baking classes at a local community college, paid for by Deener, she sees a

future at the top of the mountain.

She's reminded of it every day, right before sunrise. "It's just so beautiful," she says of her favorite spot, the big window beneath the antler chandelier. "It's so foggy it looks like an ocean, and the sky is just so red it looks like a dreamland."

— *Jeri Rowe*

Dan and Deener Matthews's cozy rooms and delectable dishes, created with fare from local farms, are all a part of the couple's mission to help guests feel "in touch with the awesomeness of creation."

RagApple Lassie Vineyards boasts a bounty of wine grapes and sweeping views of the Yadkin River Valley.

YADKIN VALLEY'S WINE COUNTRY

WESTERN N.C. | 76 miles west of Winston-Salem and beyond

RAGAPPLE LASSIE VINEYARDS, BOONVILLE

Beneath a sweeping landscape at RagApple Lassie in Boonville lie layers of tradition and innovation. The vineyard and winery are definitely a learning stretch for Frank Hobson, a third-generation tobacco farmer. The clever name — taken from one of Hobson's beloved show cows when he was a teenager — pays homage to his agricultural roots. When planning the winery construction, the Hobsons teamed up with University of North Carolina at Charlotte's School of Design. A professor at the school designed the winery to resemble common farm buildings in the area.

RagApple Lassie Vineyards
3724 RagApple Lassie Lane, Boonville
(866) RAGAPPLE
ragapplelassie.com

HANOVER PARK VINEYARD, YADKINVILLE

Originally constructed in 1897, the renovated farmhouse at Hanover Park now serves as a tasting room and winery for owners Michael and Amy Helton's labor of love. A honeymoon trip to southern France inspired the former art teachers to go into the wine business. The teachers became students, researching and learning from local sources, and they relied on their own creative background to add character. The quaint surroundings assure visitors they're in Yadkin Valley, but a sip of the wine gives a taste of the Old World.

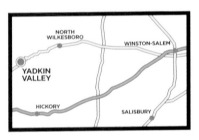

Hanover Park Vineyard
1927 Courtney-Hunts-ville Road, Yadkinville
(336) 463-2875
hanoverparkwines.com

PHOTOGRAPH BY KEVIN ADAMS

STONY KNOLL VINEYARDS, DOBSON

For the Coe family, the road always seems to lead back to the family farm. The 48-acre tract of land at Stony Knoll Vineyards, once home to tobacco instead of grapes, has been in the family since 1896. Determined to continue their farming heritage, Van Coe and his brother-in-law, Lynn Crouse, enrolled in courses at Surry Community College. With the planting of the first vines in 2001, a new family tradition was born. The landscape might have changed within the last century, but the lineage remains the same.

Stony Knoll Vineyards
1143 Stony Knoll Road, Dobson
(336) 374-5752
stonyknollvineyards.com

At Stony Knoll Vineyards, high in the rolling foothills of the Blue Ridge Mountains, the Coe family has continued their centuries-old tradition of farming the land — an estate that consists of more than five acres of planted grape varietals.

PHOTOGRAPH BY MILLIE HOLLOMAN

RAYLEN VINEYARDS AND WINERY, MOCKSVILLE

A storm is brewing inside RayLen Vineyards and Winery in Mocksville.

Expert winemaker Steve Shepard is the brains behind the winery's best seller: Category 5 — a bold wine named after the strongest hurricane. Joe and Joyce Neely transformed the 115-acre dairy farm into a vineyard and winery after inspiration and encouragement from peers in the close-knit local winemaking industry. The Neelys' enthusiasm and Shepard's experience proves to be a smart combination.

RayLen Vineyards and Winery
3577 Highway 158, Mocksville
(336) 998-3100
raylenvineyards.com

In late summer, when grapes begin to color, workers at RayLen cut and drop bunches to the ground. Their goal: quality, not just quantity. With fewer bunches, the vine produces grapes, and ultimately wine, with more body and flavor.

PHOTOGRAPHS BY SHAWN JENNINGS

SHELTON VINEYARDS, DOBSON

Brothers Charlie and Ed Shelton spent their childhood a few miles down the road from the old dairy farm, so when the land came up for auction, they purchased it. In 2009, the 200-acre vineyard celebrated its 10-year anniversary. Throughout the decade, the Sheltons have developed a successful business and a contagious passion that continues to spread throughout the region and shape the future: In 2010, Surry Community College broke ground for the construction of a state-of-the-art viticulture center, named the Shelton-Badgett North Carolina Center for Viticulture and Enology, in honor of the family of Charlie and Ed Shelton.

Shelton Vineyards
286 Cabernet Lane, Dobson
(336) 366-4724
sheltonvineyards.com

Beginning as a hobby, Shelton Vineyards is now the largest family-owned estate winery in North Carolina. Visitors can sip and swirl at the tasting bar, catch an outdoor concert, and pick up a picnic at the onsite restaurant (or bring your own).

PHOTOGRAPH COURTESY OF SHELTON VINEYARDS

ROUND PEAK VINEYARDS, MOUNT AIRY

At Round Peak Vineyards, good friends and good wine are a common combination. College friends George Little and Lee Martin took a vacation to California with their wives in 1998 and returned to Mount Airy inspired. The next year, the couples bought land for a vineyard. After courses at Surry Community College, the Littles and Martins developed their own winery in 2005. Ken Gulaian and Kari Heerdt bought the winery a few years later and have been focused on crafting wine best enjoyed among friends.

Round Peak Vineyards
765 Round Peak Church Road, Mount Airy
(336) 998-3100
roundpeak.com

Every weekend in warmer months, the back deck at Round Peak Vineyards is open, and the grill is on. Bring your bike or canine friend, and spend a relaxing day exploring the 12 acres of French and Italian varietals.

PHOTOGRAPHS BY BRIAN GOMSAK

WESTBEND VINEYARDS, LEWISVILLE

Appropriately situated in Lewisville, where the Yadkin Valley begins, Westbend Vineyards — the oldest vineyard in North Carolina — serves as an entrance to the heart of North Carolina wine country.

Westbend Vineyards began as an experiment almost 40 years ago when Jack and Lillian Kroustalis went against the advice of many agricultural experts and planted grapes grown mainly in Europe. The rebellion paid off. The Kroustalises relied on the resources at hand, converting a horse stable into a winery and using a curve in the Yadkin River as a namesake. Today, a sample of Westbend's award-winning wine produced by winemaker Mark Terry makes you thankful the Kroustalises didn't follow instructions.

Westbend Vineyards
5394 Williams Road, Lewisville
(336) 945-5032
westbendvineyards.com

— Leah Hughes

In the rolling hills where the Yadkin Valley begins, Westbend Vineyards devotes 60 of its 100 acres to growing vinifera varietals. Since the estate's first vineyard was planted in 1972, grapes used to produce California and French wines (such as Chardonnay, Riesling, and Merlot) have been thriving here on the banks of the Yadkin River.

DURHAM

CENTRAL N.C. | 28 miles northwest of Raleigh | **DURHAM-NC.COM**

Nearly all the gritty history of Durham — its boxcars loaded with golden leaves, its sweat-stained workers in white aprons, its tycoons, its jobs, its boom, its money, its heartbreak — can be traced to the redbrick warehouses of American Tobacco.

Here, you'll find the ghosts of men who saw riches glowing at the end of a cigarette, namely James Buchanan Duke, who once manufactured 90 percent of all smokes dangling from American lips.

You'll hear stories about grandparents who spent their lives inside these hot and dusty buildings, shaking leaves off stems, stuffing Lucky Strikes into packs, filling up lunch buckets with rum-soaked cigarettes that had fallen on the floor.

You'll see sepia-toned pictures of farmers gone to market to collect a season's pay, pockets suddenly bulging with money, elbowing their way through a crowd of appliance dealers, snake-oil salesmen, and baby-kissing politicians.

And you'll know that when the American Tobacco Company abandoned Durham in 1987, taking much of downtown business with it, the city swept a century into the ashcan, grumbling about the surgeon general, puffing on a Lucky.

But perhaps the most fascinating chapter in Durham's history is unfolding now inside those same buildings, which sat empty for more than a decade. The irony isn't lost on anyone that tobacco, which for so long helped fuel the Bull City's image as a haven for sin, is providing a new wave of lifeblood.

SPARKING A NEW IDEA

Reborn as the American Tobacco Campus, the warehouses that once held cigarette-rolling machines now house top software firms, advertising agencies, public radio, and a culinary school. Burt's Bees keeps its headquarters here, bringing American Tobacco full circle from carcinogens to organic balms.

From the Lucky Strike smokestack, it's a short walk to the Durham Bulls Athletic Park, or the arm-long beer menu at Tyler's Restaurant & Taproom, or the new Durham Performing Arts Center, which lures shows right off Broadway. Today, there's nothing inherently unhealthy about

A quarter-mile artificial river runs through the redesigned American Tobacco Campus, adding ambience for employees and visitors.

PHOTOGRAPHY BY NICK PIRONIO

the campus, unless you count the bleu-cheese-and-bacon burger at Tyler's or the steak chimichurri at Cuban Revolution Restaurant & Bar. It's unlikely the surgeon general will ever weigh in on the earth-friendly products made by Burt's Bees, which moved to American Tobacco last year.

And instead of dirty workers just off the assembly line, you'll find brainy tech-nerds inside wide-open offices walled with glass. Exposed ductwork runs everywhere, and inside the Powerhouse building, the walkways snake around a colossal coal furnace. Occupancy on the million-plus square-foot campus now stands at 99 percent.

They say that when an odd breeze blows through, you can still smell a trace of the sweet leaf that piled inside these buildings. The smells, the sweat, and the fortunes created here never really left. It doesn't take much to imagine them sitting on the lawn for Back Porch Music on Friday, clocking out for a few hours to enjoy the show. — *Josh Shaffer*

A recognizable entrance, a stationary railcar, and Tyler's Restaurant & Taproom all helped build a scene that generates regular foot traffic to the American Tobacco Campus.

HOW TO EXPERIENCE DURHAM:

1. Root for the home team at a **Durham Bulls baseball game**, where you might catch a fly ball or a glimpse of the team's energetic mascot, Wool E. Bull.

Durham Bulls Athletic Park
409 Blackwell Street
Durham, N.C. 27701
(919) 956-2855

2. Everything's local when you dine on campus. You've got your pick of restaurants at the American Tobacco Campus, from **Saladelia Cafe**, where you can feast on organic produce grown by Durham farmers to live jazz by local artists. Try the famous chicken salad on kaiser or rosemary salmon steaks. At **Cuban Revolution Restaurant & Bar**, the decor and music take you back to the '60s when whispers about the Rat Pack, Marilyn, and a revolutionary Cuba filled the air. And grab a drink if you can choose from the list of 60 craft and specialty import beers on tap at **Tyler's Restaurant & Taproom.** For dinner, try comfort food favorites like chicken fried chicken with braised mustard greens, mashed potatoes, and peppery white gravy.

American Tobacco Campus
318 Blackwell Street
Durham, N.C. 27701
(919) 433-1560

3. Wander the shops at Brightleaf Square, the anchor of the historic Brightleaf District. Repurposed 1904 brick tobacco warehouses now house a bevy of art galleries, jewelers, and clothing boutiques.

Brightleaf Square
Gregson Street at Main Street
Durham, N.C. 27701
(919) 682-9229

4. Catch a show from Broadway favorites like *Wicked* and *West Side Story* to concerts by Dolly Parton and Steely Dan, all at the **Durham Performing Arts Center**. You can even take the stage — just sign up online for a behind-the-scenes tour.

Durham Performing Arts Center
123 Vivian Street
Durham, N.C. 27701
(919) 688-3722

5. History Buffs won't want to miss a tour of **Bennett Place**. This simple farmhouse was the location of the largest troop surrender of the Civil War in April 1865.

Bennett Place
4409 Bennett Memorial Road
Durham, N.C. 27705
(919) 383-4345

6. Rest your feet with an old-fashioned, horse-drawn carriage ride by **Bull City Carriage Company**. Complete with a half-hour tour of the historic Brightleaf District and Duke University's East Campus.

Bull City Carriage Company
Corner of Main and Gregson streets
Durham, N.C. 27701
(919) 730-7586

7. Rent a canoe or kayak, and explore the Eno River guided by expert naturalists and historians. Night owls can paddle under the stars to learn about the night sky.

Frog Hollow Outdoors
Durham, N.C.
(919) 416-1200

NATURE IN THE CITY

Thousands of miles of rivers course across North Carolina. Some crash over rocks and through gorges in a remote mountain wilderness, while others stir through unpopulated swamps on their way to the sea. Banks Dixon, a river guide and owner of Frog Hollow Outdoors in Durham, organizes trips on both ends of the spectrum. But he also champions our state's more developed areas. Like the Triangle, where the last bit of wilderness tends to linger along the rivers.

"I constantly have folks who are surprised. They're like, 'Wow! This is right in my backyard?'" he says.

The Triangle's "backyard" sits in two river basins — the Neuse and the Cape Fear. And several smaller rivers snake their way toward these main branches. There's the Eno, the Flat, the Haw, and the Deep. You just have to know where to get on them. That's where having a guide who's been navigating Piedmont waterways since he was a teenager comes in handy.

For Dixon, any day on a river is a good day, but his best days are when he sees someone start to love paddling as much as he does. He sees it in their body language. On the shore, they're tight, reserved. Then they get some instruction and start to melt into their surroundings.

"It's just being in a space where there aren't cars zooming by; there's not the buzz of the city," Dixon says. "People start to relax into those connections, and you can see all the stress of daily life shed away."

SHEER BEAUTY

Dixon, who met his wife, Andrea, on the Appalachian Trail and later proposed to her while they hiked Annapurna 3 in Nepal, marvels at the peace to be found within yards of some of the Triangle's busiest thruways.

An hour on this abbreviated river link is enough time for him to impress visitors with what there is to love out here. Like the sense you're in the middle of nowhere; West Point on the Eno Park sits on 388 mostly wild acres.

Dixon could spend all day out here and not run out of insights to share. He might talk about the wildlife you're likely to encounter — deer and turtles, eagles and beavers. At other stops, he describes the different seasons on a Piedmont river. And he takes time to slow down, simply to appreciate the tranquility, the beauty of woods not quite clear of winter, exposed branches and bark jagged and arresting.

All this on less than two miles of river.

— *Diane Summerville*

HOW TO EXPERIENCE THE ENO:

Frog Hollow Outdoors
To register for a trip, call
(919) 416-1200

All paths lead to the water for Banks Dixon, a Durham river guide.

SAXAPAHAW

CENTRAL N.C. | 16 miles southeast of Burlington | **SAXAPAHAW.COM**

In lower Alamance County, where the Haw River runs, you'll find an old gym with puppets the size of pickup trucks and a concrete-floor basement where you can rent enough kayaks, canoes, and pirogues to create your own navy.

Then, up 41 stone steps across the street, you'll spy a bulletin board outside the post office that offers almost anything — from where to repair quilts and buy Pomeranian puppies to how to meditate like a Chinese monk.

You can read the fine print of 13 paragraphs and see how clean the local water is. Or you can simply listen, and you'll hear people sharing first names and good stories. And that's when you'll get it. This is Saxapahaw.

THE MODERN MILL VILLAGE

Like all mill towns hugging the rivers of North Carolina, Saxapahaw faced a tough future. After 150 years of spinning cotton into yarn, the mill closed in 1994. Dixie Yarns was the last owner.

The reasons for the closure are all too familiar in North Carolina: rising costs, cheap labor overseas, and the changing tastes of a buying public.

John McLean Jordan Jr. — everyone calls him Mac — loved that mill. His grandfather, the late U.S. Senator B. Everett Jordan, bought the mill in 1927 with the help of his uncle and ran it for nearly 50 years. In 1994, Mac convinced his father, John Jordan, to buy back the 31 acres and the 250,000-square-foot mill after Dixie Yarns left.

John did, for $385,000.

Before that, John had bought and renovated more than 60 mill-village homes, and established a foundation to help those locally in need. Yet still, John had another idea for this mill in need.

He placed his oldest son in charge.

Today, the Saxapahaw Rivermill is a cavernous maze of apartments and condominiums, with a center for fitness and healing.

ALL ROADS LEAD TO SAXAPAHAW

Although it's difficult to say "Saxapahaw," the name is as old as North Carolina itself.

After John Jordan (center) purchased the Saxapahaw Rivermill in 1994, he put his son, Mac (right), in charge of making something out of it. Mac asked his brother, Carter (left), to come home and help.

SAXAPAHAW

In 1569, a Spanish explorer visited the early settlers of the lower Alamance, the Sissipahaw Indians, and described this land beside the Haw as "Sauxpa."

Around 1700, an English explorer gave the area a description a little easier to pronounce: the "flower of Carolina." But during the past few decades, this crossroads has been saddled with another name: UCLA.

Or Upper Chatham, Lower Alamance.

There was a time when folks made fun of UCLA. Not anymore. Today, UCLA is coveted for its affordable real estate, its laid-back lifestyle, and its proximity to places like Chapel Hill, Elon, and Research Triangle Park.

Every Saturday from May through August, a hillside beside the post office turns into an old-school example of social networking — a farmers market of food, art, and homegrown music.

"You know, all roads lead to Saxapahaw," people will tell you.

You'll hear that at the Saxapahaw General Store. It's true. Saxapahaw has all sorts of names now: "west Chapel Hill," "mini-Asheville," and of course, UCLA.

This community well off Interstate 40, with no stoplight, is a place where new merges with old, organically creating a community all its own.

The Saxapahaw General Store is a three-aisle spot that can seat 35 on the inside. Two gas pumps are out front, an armload of firewood props open the front door, and a flier near the counter advertises a class for barefoot ballroom dancing.

On this particular Saturday, two kids poke at each other while their dad orders the store's specialty on a house-made English muffin, with Manchego cheese, roasted tomatoes, lemon garlic aioli, and an olive tapenade. It's the Saxapahaw Goat Burger.

It's the creation of Jeff Barney. He's the guy behind the counter in the "Feel Me, I'm Organic" T-shirt.

He runs Saxapahaw General Store with his partner, Cameron Ratliff. They have replaced milk crates with patio furniture and assist people interested in buying what Barney calls "peasant food from around the world."

Together, they have turned an old convenience store into a culinary magnet.

"I like this place because there is not a lot of stuff," a customer told Barney once. "It's not stuffy."

And that is Saxapahaw. It exudes this aw-shucks earnestness where everyone here will turn a parking lot, an aisle, or even the bulletin board beside the post office into a conversation spot. — *Jeri Rowe*

Have lunch at the Saxapahaw General Store, run by Jeff Barney and Cameron Ratliff (opposite, top left). We recommend the Goat Burger (bottom left), which Barney created himself.

Donovan Zimmerman (left) co-founded Paperhand Puppet Intervention in the old gym.

HOW TO EXPERIENCE SAXAPAHAW:

1. In the summer, Saturdays in Saxapahaw is an ideal time to get a feel for this little village and its friendly people. Each weekend from May to August, vendors line the hill with produce and baked goods, and live music fills the air. Festivities begin at 5 p.m., and the evening wraps up around 8 p.m.

2. Relax with a full-body massage or a yoga class at **The Bridge at Rivermill**, a healing and fitness center. You can even weigh-in on the mill's original cotton scale.

Saxapahaw Rivermill
1616 Jordan Drive
Saxapahaw, N.C. 27340
(336) 376-3122

3. Grab a bite to eat with locals at **Saxapahaw General Store.** Try a bowl of house-made chili with duck fat fries — or daily specials, like tuna au poivre.

Saxapahaw General Store
1735 Saxapahaw-Bethlehem Church Road
Saxapahaw, N.C. 27340
(336) 376-5332

4. Venture to the Haw River in the heart of town. Explore by land with public walking trails or by water. Bring your kayak, canoe, or swimsuit and jump in.

Saxapahaw Rivermill
1616 Jordan Drive
Saxapahaw, N.C. 27340
(336) 376-3122

ILLUSTRATION BY STEVEN NOBLE

Deceptively serene,
The Umstead's poolside cabanas
are wired for work.

THE UMSTEAD HOTEL AND SPA

CENTRAL N.C. | 11 miles west of Raleigh | **THEUMSTEAD.COM**

D r. Jim and Ann Goodnight didn't start out with the idea of building a luxury hotel. But when Morley Safer from "60 Minutes" came to town to interview Jim, his only option was a nearby suites hotel. The Goodnights, the majority owners of SAS, the largest privately held software company in the world, realized then that the Triangle needed a high-end hotel.

Jim was a student in the statistics department at North Carolina State University in the late 1960s when he started working on a project to increase crop yields. He helped develop software that analyzed large amounts of data collected through the United States Department of Agriculture. The software was referred to as "statistical analysis system" or SAS.

Soon, other industries recognized the value of computerized systems analysis; the program eventually developed software for pharmaceutical and insurance companies. But in the 1970s, universities weren't prepared to convert academics into commercial endeavors. So in 1976, with their superiors' blessings, Jim, by then an assistant professor, and his partners established SAS as a private enterprise. They rented office space in Hillsborough and started up with nearly 100 corporate, academic, and government clients. Within two years, the company was serving 600 sites and, in 1980, broke ground on its first building.

Today, SAS employs nearly 11,000 people worldwide. In Cary, it owns 900 acres and has developed roughly 350 of them — so far.

By the early 2000s, the Triangle was primed for a high-end hotel. When the Goodnights saw the need, their first impulse was to recruit a five-star hotel, not start one on their own. They approached the Ritz-Carlton first, and then the Four Seasons. Both resorts declined.

"When Jim called the Four Seasons," Ann says, "they told him, 'Quite frankly, if we sent one of our managers to a hotel in Cary, North Carolina, they would interpret that as a demotion.'"

Their Tar Heel pride was a bit wounded, but the Goodnights understood.

"We are evolving," Ann says of the region. "We just try to push it a little bit more than the rest of the world believes we can."

The Umstead Hotel and Spa, which opened in January 2007, is part of the push to be more.

Guests here find themselves surrounded

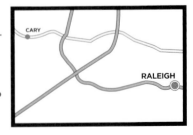

Guests here find themselves surrounded by luxury and a full contingent of people dedicated to their contentment.

by luxury and a full contingent of people dedicated to their contentment. In the spa, you can receive a Babassu Sugar Scrub, The Umstead Body Ritual, or any of a host of services to slow the pulse. Dinner at Herons, the hotel's gourmet restaurant, is a transformative experience built around such creative dishes as strawberry gazpacho with a hint of jalapeno and rhubarb soup poured over lemongrass custard.

There's tea in the parlor every afternoon at 3 p.m.; strains from a harpist's or guitarist's hands add a soothing note to the refined atmosphere. In the evening, a piano player lightens the mood as patrons unwind in the bar. Tastings on the Terrace encourage hotel guests and visitors from the community to unwind in a garden setting.

Throughout the hotel, the Umstead boasts an art collection that honors not

The Umstead's outdoor spaces offer a restful setting overlooking the gardens and pond.

Opposite: The prize piece in The Umstead's art collection — *Ardea Figura* by Dale Chihuly. And, in the guest rooms, sumptuous linens add to the luxury.

only the natural setting but several North Carolina and Southeastern artists, including North Carolina pottery icons Ben Owen III and Mark Hewitt.

The prize piece in The Umstead's art collection — *Ardea Figura* by the internationally acclaimed Dale Chihuly — rises in crystalline stems out of a mossy bed in the lounge. Overhead lighting shimmers on the rippled glass, creating an illusion of movement, as if a breeze is nudging the clear tendrils arching skyward.

In its unaltered form, glass is sharp and straight edged, a functional material used to block the elements or admit light. In Chihuly's hands, it softens, comes to life, and yields to the artist's imagination, which stretches and bends and transforms it into emotion. As it cools, the glass reverts to its solid state, apparently flowing yet motionless, a blend of intensity and stillness.

And it becomes a fitting centerpiece for a place where high-powered professionals go to find peace. — *Diane Summerville*

The Umstead Hotel and Spa
100 Woodland Pond Drive
Cary, N.C. 27513
(866) 877-4141

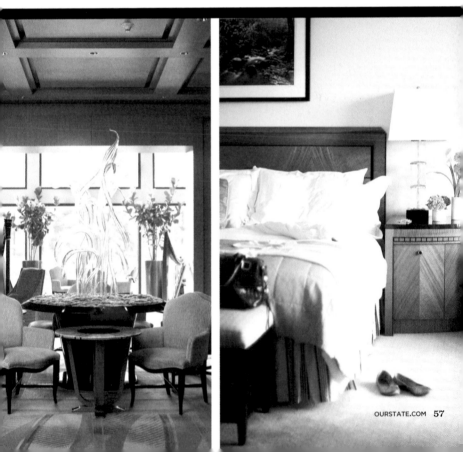

ASHEBORO

For a time during the 20th century, the city in the center of Randolph County billed itself as the center of the state. The U.S. Army Corps of Engineers killed that public relations campaign in 1989, announcing that satellite readings had instead pinpointed the Montgomery County town of Star as the state's geographic center.

Geographically speaking, Asheboro may be slightly off center, but major highways pass through it from the cardinal points of the compass: U.S. Highway 64, N.C. Highway 49, and U.S. Highway 220 (the future route of Interstates 73/74). Charlotte, the state's largest city, is an hour's drive to the southwest; Raleigh, the state capital, is an hour to the east. Local officials are banking on location as one catalyst for future growth. So is the N.C. Zoo, which counts visitors by the hundreds of thousands. City council member Linda Carter envisions giant elephant footprints stenciled on main roads into town, trumpeting the fact that Asheboro is home to the largest walkthrough natural habitat zoo in the world.

The city is blessed with other unique tourist destinations.

The American Classic Motorcycle Company, on U.S. Highway 64 West, houses a shop, a diner, and one of the world's largest privately owned collections of Harley-Davidson motorcycles. Hungry folks can order flywheels (waffles), saddlebags (side orders), and low riders (salads). The North Carolina Aviation Museum at Asheboro Regional Airport, on Pilots View Road off N.C. Highway 49, houses about a dozen aircraft (historic, experimental, and unmanned), including a Piper Cub flown by Orville Wright, and a collection of military memorabilia that spans World War I, World War II, Korea, Vietnam, and the Cold War.

The city's evolving downtown revitalization began with a public-private partnership to demolish an old bus station to make way for Bicentennial Park. The Asheboro and Randolph Rotary clubs contributed money to add a roof to the park's concrete-and-brick stage. Now, a few Sunday evenings every summer, music lovers meet on the green expanse for free concerts.

The city also bought The Sunset Theatre, a 1930s-era movie house, and two buildings next to it, with plans to

James and Carol Rich enjoy a stroll along Sunset Avenue, where the center of downtown teems with local businesses.

A few Sunday evenings every summer, music lovers meet on the green expanse for free concerts.

create a performing arts center. With a few cosmetic upgrades and the addition of a digital marquee, the downtown landmark draws thousands for concerts, movies, and plays each year. — *Chip Womick*

HOW TO EXPERIENCE ASHEBORO:

1. Lift your spirits. Across the railroad tracks in downtown Asheboro is **The Flying Pig**, a small eatery that became a destination for local folks the day it opened in June 2009. Late at night, the sound of music spills out through the doorway each time a customer comes or goes. Inside, the walls are decorated with jerseys, banners, and other paraphernalia for high school, college, and professional teams. Bring in something touting your team, says Barry Yow, one of the proprietors, and they'll find a place for it.

Every seat is filled. Customers crowd shoulder-to-shoulder around the bar. Yow and his wife, Mary Ann, and their friends, Dennis and Barbara Gallimore, own and operate the restaurant and bar. Often during a friendship that spans two decades, Barry and Dennis talked about partnering in a venture, although they differed on the vision. Yow wanted to open a little bar; Gallimore, a pizzeria serving hand-tossed pies made using his secret recipe for dough.

When voters approved the sale of beverage alcohol in the summer of 2008 — ending 50 years of local prohibition — the men and their wives melded these dreams into an establishment named to commemorate a long-held notion: Alcohol would be legalized in Asheboro when pigs fly.

The Flying Pig
208 Sunset Avenue
Asheboro, N.C. 27203
(336) 610-3737

2. And speaking of pigs, get a glimpse of the red river hogs in the Bushlands area at the **North Carolina Zoo.** More than 200 species of animals, including polar bears, zebras, and lemurs, are on display at one of the finest natural-habitat zoos in the nation.

North Carolina Zoo
4401 Zoo Parkway
Asheboro, N.C. 27205
(800) 488-0444
nczoo.org

Because voters approved the end of local prohibition in 2008, folks can openly have a pizza and a beer at a place appropriately named "The Flying Pig."
Opposite, top left: Circa Gallery on Sunset Avenue draws plenty of foot traffic coming to see the artistic creations.
Opposite, bottom left: Volunteers give a mural entitled "Randolph Memories," originally painted in 1976, in downtown Asheboro a fresh coat of paint.

An artist's rendering illustrates the close connection between indoor and outdoor spaces at the new museum.

N.C. MUSEUM OF ART

CENTRAL N.C. | Raleigh | **NCARTMUSEUM.ORG**

For decades, the North Carolina Museum of Art showed off its treasures inside a brown brick box — a featureless rectangle that looked half like a high school and half like a bunker. Inside, the paintings were crowded together, often downstairs in dim and windowless chambers, so the experience of seeing Monet felt like rooting through your uncle's basement.

Today, Museum Director Larry Wheeler stands at the front door of his $84 million expansion and gestures grandly to the rows of birches and magnolias, the fountains, the pond with floating lily pads, and the spot at the front door reserved for Rodin.

He swoons when he describes the building's silvery skin made of anodized aluminum, which reflects the waving tree branches and the passing clouds.

And when he opens the front door, you see soft, filtered sunlight pouring in through floor-to-ceiling windows.

A NICE PLACE TO SIT

It's rare that a building in North Carolina goes up with a philosophy, with an ambition, or with anything more in mind than keeping out the rain. But this one comes with the challenge of connecting man-made art to natural beauty, of showing ordinary taxpayers that

The idea: Build a place so peaceful, so thought-provoking, so picturesque that you'd want to visit even if you couldn't tell Andrew Wyeth from Wyatt Earp.

Greek sculpture and willow trees make a nice combination, that Renaissance paintings look good against a backdrop of Blue Ridge Mountain boulders.

The idea: Build a place so peaceful, so thought-provoking, so picturesque that you'd want to visit even if you couldn't tell Andrew Wyeth from Wyatt Earp. It is simply a nice place to sit.

"The central notion," Wheeler explains, "was if we could make people come into this building, they would be both comforted and uplifted by the experience. Or, if they didn't want to look at art, they could have a cup of coffee and sit with Rodin sculptures."

In New York, Washington, or Chicago, an art museum stands on a crowded city block with cabs honking and buses whooshing past. You can get there on a subway. But North Carolina hung its paintings and stood its sculptures in the middle of 164 acres of grass and trees.

Walking through the space, you're surrounded by glass. The rocks, leaves, and water outside are on display as much as the giant Robert Motherwell abstract, and your eyes roll over all of them at once.

This building celebrates both the handmade and God-made varieties of beauty. It shows off stone cut with a chisel and stone pulled out of the ground.

And it fills its halls with real light. Half the museum's walls are glass, and more

light floats down from recessed skylights.

Wheeler wanted the pictures glowing under it, so that when visitors look at a Madonna and Child painted in the 14th century, the gold leaf would shine like it did for Giotto as he created it.

Wheeler wanted a place that felt like North Carolina — that reflected its working-class, everyman identity. He didn't want a snobbish place, or one that required an art history degree to enjoy.

The art isn't forced on anyone here. There's no set path through this museum, and there's hardly any explanation of the works.

If you want a history of European painting through the centuries, it's available on headphones. But Wheeler isn't going to push it on you with huge blocks of text.

The point at this museum isn't to fixate on one piece, then another, but to examine them all together, equalized against a white background like children playing in the snow.

Come for the expansion, for the bright silver, tall glass, and peaceful lighting. And as your eyes wander over the centuries, you'll add to North Carolina's collection, just by being there to enjoy it. — *Josh Shaffer*

Art isn't contained solely within the airy, opaque-glass building. Outdoor installations dot the premises.

HOW TO EXPERIENCE THE N.C. MUSEUM OF ART:

1. **Take a free, guided tour** of West Building and get an introduction to the Museum's collection. No reservations necessary; meet at the West Building Information Desk.

2. **Interact with art** in the **Museum Park**. More than 160 acres of fields, woodlands, and creeks where you can bike or stroll — and even bring your canine friend. Don't miss the Cloud Chamber, a 12-foot structure that acts as a giant pinhole camera pointed at the sky, and take note of *Invasive*, the temporary "road tattoos" painted on the sidewalks and trails.

3. **During the summer months** the Museum Park is home to dozens of outdoor concerts and movies. Catch screenings of current releases like *King's Speech* or old favorites like *Back to the Future*.

4. **Bring the kids along** and see children's performances of classic storybook tales or drop-in for free, hands-on craft workshops. Make your own portrait or see larger-than-life dragon puppets take over the park. Space is limited; sign up in advance.

5. **Indulge all of your senses** at **Iris**, a full-service, onsite restaurant. Sample seasonal cuisine (like braised beef short rib potpie with root vegetables) as you gaze out the floor-to-ceiling windows for a view of the surrounding gardens. And don't skip dessert — treats like pumpkin and pecan creme brulee with toasted rosemary marshmallows fill the menu — and your belly.

6. **Browse the Museum Store** to find take-home treasures, such as Seagrove pottery vases and carved resin bangles. Shop tax-free; all proceeds benefit the programming and operation of the museum. Added bonus: Become a member of the museum and save 10 percent on all purchases.

North Carolina Museum of Art
2110 Blue Ridge Road
Raleigh, N.C. 27607
(919) 839-6262

14 CHARLOTTE

CENTRAL N.C. | 92 miles southwest of Greensboro | **CHARLOTTESGOTALOT.COM**

When people think of shopping in or around Charlotte, it's easy to picture the usual suspects. There's Concord Mills, North Carolina's No. 1 visitor attraction, with more than 200 stores, including the only Bass Pro Shops in the state. Then there's SouthPark with retail jewels Neiman Marcus, Tiffany & Co., and Louis Vuitton. However, if you look beyond the glitz and glamour of the Queen City, you'll discover a shopping experience that is just that — an experience. Throughout the area, old and not-so-old places offer a taste of the region's history with an extra helping of Southern hospitality.

GREATER CHARLOTTE ANTIQUE AND COLLECTIBLES SHOW

For folks who don't like to fill their homes with cookie-cutter furnishings, the Greater Charlotte Antique and Collectibles Show, a five-time-a-year event, tempts with one-of-a-kind finds.

"There are young people that look for good quality antiques," says Lydia Sullivan, show manager, adding that the show has more than 200 vendors. "We have such a mixed demographic. … Primarily it's women shoppers at antique shows, but there are men collectors, too."

There's lots of collecting to be done at this show, which recently moved from Metrolina Tradeshow Expo in Charlotte, where it had been for 38 years, to make a fresh start at the Cabarrus Arena and Events Center in Concord. "We're going to have some really good country primitives, some very high-end porcelains and silver, [and] fine art," Sullivan says. "There will still be a lot of war memorabilia and political paper."

But, as the vendors will tell you, the show is about more than stuff. "We just love antiques," says Carole Harper, who exhibits at the show with her husband, Jay, and their company, American Spirit Antiques.

THE MINT MUSEUM SHOP

A rainbow of Spanish scarves hangs on a long partition wall in the middle of The Mint Museum of Craft and Design shop. Not far away is a basket of $3.50 cardboard masks, including one of Mona Lisa, beside

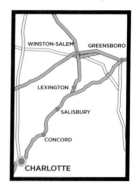

Charlotte's urban park, a 1.5-acre expanse surrounded by local businesses, is an excellent place to take a quick break from shopping.

"People buy memories. They want to take something home that's locally made."

a rack of shirts that read, "Don't Drink and Draw." Across the store, glass pieces by Spruce Pine's Valerie and Rick Beck sparkle on shelves.

The whimsical order of the shop can be attributed to the merchandising and display talents of Sandy Fisher and her staff. As manager and buyer of retail operations, Fisher knows what people are looking for: "People buy memories. They want to take something home that's locally made." Many of the items in the 2,000-square-foot shop are locally made, but there are also other criteria involved in making Fisher's cut. "The merchandise, of course, must always relate to the museum's collection and special exhibitions," she says.

"You get to make people enjoy their visit to the museum. You help people learn something they didn't know," she says. "What can be more fun than that?" — *Lori Tate*

HOW TO EXPERIENCE CHARLOTTE:

1. After a day of shopping, you'll need a place to rest. Listed on the National Register of Historic Places, the **Duke Mansion Inn** was once the home of James Buchanan Duke. In Charlotte's uptown, the fully restored, circa-1929 **Dunhill Hotel**, is a great choice for its historical feel. And for something on the upper end of the spectrum, try the luxurious **Ritz-Carlton**.

Duke Mansion Inn
400 Hermitage Road
Charlotte, N.C. 28207
(704) 714-4400
dukemansion.com

Dunhill Hotel
237 North Tryon Street
Charlotte, N.C. 28202
(704) 332-4141
dunhillhotel.com

Ritz-Carlton
201 East Trade Street
Charlotte, N.C. 28202
(704) 547-2244
ritzcarlton.com

2. Ready to eat? We love **Mert's Heart and Soul** for its Southern-style menu that includes Low Country and Gullah favorites, and the western-style **Old Hickory House Restaurant** is a step back in time to when North Tryon Street was the main route to Richmond, Virginia.

Mert's Heart and Soul
214 North College Street
Charlotte, N.C. 28202
mertscharlotte.com

Old Hickory House Restaurant
6538 North Tryon Street
Charlotte, N.C. 28213
(704) 596-8014

3. Hop aboard Charlotte's Lynx Blue Line, a user-friendly light-rail system traversing the Center City. You can buy tickets with cash or credit at each stop along the line; ticket prices range from 75 cents for a student and senior one-way ticket to $15 for a seven-day pass.

Lynx Blue Line
214 North College Street
Charlotte, N.C. 28202
(704) 336-7433
lynxcharlotte.com

4. Take in sky-high views of the city skyline aboard a hot-air balloon. **Balloons Over Charlotte** has flown two flights a day, seven days a week for the past 20 years.

Balloons Over Charlotte
3709 Sweetgrass Lane
Charlotte, N.C. 28226
(704) 541-7058

5. Visit the Levine Center for the Arts, a cultural campus that includes the **Bechtler Museum of Modern Art** (home to pieces by artists from Picasso to Warhol) and the newly opened **Mint Museum Uptown**, known for its collections of contemporary art and stunning architecture.

Bechtler Museum of Modern Art
420 South Tryon Street
Charlotte, N.C. 28202
(704) 353-9200
bechtler.org

Mint Museum Uptown
500 South Tryon Street
Charlotte, N.C. 28202
(704) 337-2000
mintmuseum.org

The Greater Charlotte Antiques and Collectibles Show promises a bounty of one-of-a-kind finds (opposite, top left). Grab a quick lunch at Matt's Chicago Dog (bottom left), take a seat outside, and soak up Charlotte's city atmosphere.

15

KILL DEVIL HILLS

EASTERN N.C. | 202 miles east of Raleigh | **KDHNC.COM**

The sun rises, casting a yellow glow onto the Wright brothers monument that towers 60 feet above this town. The propellers on the wind turbine over the Outer Banks Brewing Station hum lazily in a light southwest wind. Walkers amble along the beach, and on Bay Drive, children set up camp in the sand with buckets and shovels, and anglers throw squid-stuffed hooks from the wooden, wave-worn Avalon Pier.

Out on the bypass highway, a minivan on the way to day care passes another minivan headed to Stack 'Em High for waffles. Merchants unlock shop doors, and prep cooks chop vegetables for the lunch rush. Dogs wait outside at the Front Porch Cafe while their owners, wearing flip-flops, order lattes from the suntanned baristas inside.

It's another summer morning in the town of Kill Devil Hills — KDH, we call it. Part hometown, part vacation destination, this is a beach town through and through.

TOWN WITH ENERGY

Perhaps the one thing that Kill Devil Hills should be known for, it isn't. Nationwide, the Wright brothers are synonymous with Kitty Hawk, the town just north of here. They arrived on the Outer Banks at Kitty Hawk, and they postmarked all their mail from the Kitty Hawk Post Office. But in fact, the actual location of the brothers' first flight was just south, on Big Kill Devil Hill, in what is now the town of Kill Devil Hills. Back then, Big Kill Devil Hill was a part of a sprawling system of sand dunes similar to Nags Head's Jockey's Ridge. The soft sand was the perfect spot for those flying experiments. The sand hill was later planted with stabilizing grass, and a concrete pylon monument to the brothers was completed there in 1932. The monument, now part of the 314-acre Wright Brothers National Memorial, is the center and definitive focal point of Kill Devil Hills.

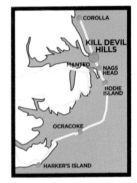

There are many theories about how Kill Devil Hills got its name. One of the more popular stories is that it originated from a brand of rum, called Kill Devil Rum.

PHOTOGRAPHY BY ELIZABETH ZONGOLOWICZ

Within sight of that monument is another, newer symbolic structure — a wind turbine at Outer Banks Brewing Station. The owners of the popular restaurant and brewery erected the wind turbine in 2008 to become the first wind-powered brewpub in the nation. The turbine doesn't generate all of the power the restaurant uses, but it does deflect some of the cost of the power bill. It's also an interesting sight in town, an attention magnet for the restaurant, a way to gauge the ever-present wind conditions, and a conversation starter about green energy.

"It gets people talking about alternative sources of energy while they're enjoying a beer," says co-owner Aubrey Davis. A weather station atop the turbine is tied into data-gathering groups at two North Carolina universities, and in the restaurant's lounge, patrons can pull up data on weather and the power that the turbine is generating.

'BEST QUALITY OF LIFE'
In 2009, *Surfer* magazine put the town on its list of the Ten Best Surf Towns in

America, and it was the waves that brought Ben Sproul to Kill Devil Hills 24 years ago. He came to wait tables and surf during and after college. "That's a common story of how people get here," says Sproul. "They come on vacation, and then they think, 'How can I get here for good?'"

With Steve Pauls, Sproul co-owns The Pit Surf Shop and Boardriders Grill, a shop, bar, and grill in a beach-cottage–style building on stilts. The Pit screams nonconventional, which is why it's been a mainstay on the surf scene for more than a decade. A stop in here is a uniquely local experience.

Sproul, a former military brat who has lived all over the world, has found his permanent home. "I thought I'd live in a big city," he says, "but this is more my speed. It's still unspoiled in a lot of ways. … It's close enough to civilization but far enough from the crowds, so you're not overrun with humanity. I'll probably stay here forever."

— *Molly Harrison*

When the Wright brothers made their first flight, they never could have imagined a town forming or a Wright Brothers National Memorial (opposite, bottom) standing here a century later.

These days, the town has plenty to offer, including the Front Porch Cafe (opposite, top left) and the Outer Banks Brewing Station, known for great beer and a wind turbine its owners Aubrey Davis and Eric Reece (left) put up to partially power the brewpub.

HOW TO EXPERIENCE KILL DEVIL HILLS:

1. Start your day with a fresh cup of joe at **Front Porch Cafe**, where the whole-bean coffee is roasted on site.

Front Porch Cafe
2200 North Croatan Highway
Kill Devil Hills, N.C. 27948
(252) 449-6616

2. Rent a board, take a surf lesson, or just sample the surf-inspired menu at **The Pit Surf Shop and Boardriders Grill.** Try a California Burrito — two hands required.

The Pit Surf Shop and Boardriders Grill
1209 South Croatan Highway
Kill Devil Hills, N.C. 27948
(252) 480-3128

3. Pull up a seat at the Outer Banks Brewing Station where you can hear live bands, locals chatting, and the hum of the wind turbine outside.

The Outer Banks Brewing Station
600 South Croatan Highway
Kill Devil Hills, N.C. 27948
(252) 449-2739

4. Support local artists at KDH Cooperative Gallery and Studios. See art in oil, ceramics, and pottery — and even buy a piece to take home.

KDH Cooperative Gallery and Studios
502 South Croatan Highway
Kill Devil Hills, N.C. 27948
(252) 441-9888

ILLUSTRATION BY STEVEN NOBLE

Capture a frame-worthy shot of Bodie Island Lighthouse, one of seven North Carolina lighthouses with photographic appeal.

16 BODIE ISLAND LIGHTHOUSE

EASTERN N.C. | 6.5 miles south of Kitty Hawk | **TOWNOFNAGSHEAD.NET**

The tower that graces the southern tip of Bodie Island today is the third to mark the spot. The first tower began operation in 1848; the second, lit in 1859, was destroyed as the Civil War drew to a close. In 1872, the black-and-white bands of the Bodie Island Lighthouse signaled a new era of safety for ships traversing the North Carolina coast.

A great place to reflect on the lighthouse and the beauty of the Outer Banks is at Coquina Beach at Bodie Island, considered one of the safest swimming beaches in the area. The National Park Service arranges visitor activities, such as gathering by evening campfires in the summer and viewing the shipwrecked remains of the Laura A. Barnes, a schooner that came ashore in 1921. And if you just want to relax and dig your toes into the sand, look for some friendly companions: Coquina Beach got its name from the coquina clams that burrow in the sand here.

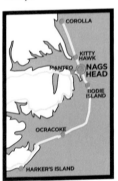

HOW TO EXPERIENCE BODIE ISLAND LIGHTHOUSE:

1. Visit the keeper's quarters. The white building nestled at the base of the lighthouse was once the keeper's quarters but has since been restored and repurposed as a visitors center. The center, open year-round, offers exhibits, a gift shop, and an Eastern National Bookstore.

2. Bring a picnic, and enjoy the view. Pack a basket of goodies, spread out a blanket, and have lunch in the shadow of the towering lighthouse. Also, an excellent photo opportunity.

3. Explore the coastal environment around you. Take a self-guided tour through the surrounding marsh with a marked nature trail and marsh board-walk. Bring your binoculars for some coastal bird-watching. See glossy ibis, herons, egrets, and other wading birds.

Bodie Island Lighthouse
Bodie Island Lighthouse Road
Nags Head, N.C. 27959
(252) 441-5711

4. Do a double-take. Head north, and make a stop by the **Currituck Beach Lighthouse** (about 40 miles up the road in Corolla), considered Bodie's architectural twin, despite their difference in coloring. The station includes a Victorian stick-style keeper's house, cisterns, and a museum shop.

Currituck Beach Lighthouse
1101 Corolla Village Road
Corolla, N.C. 27927
(252) 453-8152
currituckbeachlight.com

Cruising high over the North Carolina coast in an open cockpit gives visitors a birds-eye view of the intricacies created when land and water meet.

BIPLANE RIDE, OAK ISLAND

EASTERN N.C. | 160 miles south of Raleigh

You're flying 1,000 feet above Oak Island, with the wind pinpricking your face, you look below and see rows of houses no bigger than your thumbnail. Beach blankets look like playing cards; the Atlantic is one big painting full of greens and blues. Meanwhile, the Oak Island Pier — considered the tallest pier on the North Carolina coast at 27 feet above sea level — is as long and slender as a popsicle stick.

After a shower scrubs the sky, you can see clear to Georgetown, South Carolina. But on this particular Saturday, after weeks of no rain, the horizon is the color of expired milk, and you see only a few miles in any direction.

But the sights you see — even for a few miles — make you think like a kid again. But then, your adult self reels you in when you see some things the size of freckles on the beach. They're waving.

People. Yes, people. They see you, and you see them. They hear the chug of your seven-cylinder engine and look up to see a plane that's been burned into their memory.

You're in a biplane, 23 feet long, with a 30-foot wingspan and a 96-inch wooden propeller. The WACO UPF-7, an acronym for the Waco Aircraft Company.

She comes from another era: 1942, a trainer for pilots in World War II. But today, she rests on her three wheels at the Cape Fear Regional Jetport, a small airstrip beside the Intracoastal Waterway at Oak Island.

She's the Carolina Belle, owned by Jim and Laura Banky, husband and wife who operate Suncoast Aviation and offer scenic rides over the

Ten minutes in the air and you feel like a seagull.

marshes and beaches, lighthouses and shoals of Oak and Bald Head islands.

She does have some serious celebrity credibility, this Carolina Belle. Watch the 2002 film *Divine Secrets of the Ya-Ya Sisterhood*, and you'll see her flying above Burgaw and Buckner Hill Plantation, with Mahalia Jackson singing "Walk In Jerusalem" underneath the vroom of her engine. Actress Ashley Judd sits in her cockpit beside a young girl, looking over North Carolina.

"Isn't it just like a fairyland," Judd says. "Don't we live in the most magical place? We're like two angels up in the sky smiling down at all our friends."

Laura Banky knows that scene, and she mentions it any time the phone rings and she hears skepticism, worry, or questions on the other end.

This particular Saturday is no exception. "Biplane Rides, this is Laura. … Yes,

it's straight and level flying. No fancy maneuvers. You get to see all kinds of stuff from the air. Yes, it's an open cockpit. The wind is blowing, but there is a windscreen, so it's not right in your face. But it's like riding a motorcycle in the sky.

"You know Ashley Judd? … She rode in this biplane in the movie. That's right — *Divine Secrets of the Ya-Ya Sisterhood*. Tell them that. That always helps. I mean, if Ashley Judd can fly in it, anybody can."

Up in the air, the only sound you hear is the throaty burr-raw of the engine and the squawk from your headphones as Jim points to the many sights passing below.

There's Old Baldy. There's the Oak Island Lighthouse. There's Battery Island. And there's the Frying Pan Shoals, the last resting place of more than 130 ships.

Ten minutes in the air and you feel like a seagull, like an adventurer, and you realize, as you seemingly float on the precarious winds of the Atlantic, you don't have a care in the world.

— Jeri Rowe

Pilot Jim Banky shares his passion for flight by offering rides on the Carolina Belle. His smile widens as customers conquer their fears.

HOW TO EXPERIENCE OAK ISLAND:

1. Take the flight on with a 20- to 25-minute tour by **Suncoast Aviation**. Soar in the cockpit of the Carolina Belle as you look down over the Atlantic and the town of Oak Island.

Suncoast Aviation
4019 Long Beach Road
Oak Island, N.C. 28465
(910) 279-9476

2. Soak up some sun. The town boasts miles of sandy beaches with 65 public access points. So relax with a good book, search for shells, or hit the waves.

3. Sip and swirl more than 50 varieties from around the world with a wine tasting in the outdoor courtyard at **The Grape & Ale**.

The Grape & Ale
8521 East Oak Island Drive
Oak Island, N.C. 28465
(910) 933-4384

4. Learn about the natural wildlife at the **Oak Island Nature Center**. See live animals and wander the Talking Tree Trail. Visit the Dot Kelly Memorial Butterfly & Hummingbird Garden.

Oak Island Nature Center
5202 East Yacht Drive
Oak Island, N.C. 28465
(910) 201-1392

5. Walk the Oak Island Pier. Stroll out over the ocean, and see fishermen with their latest catch.

Oak Island Pier
705 Ocean Drive
Oak Island, N.C. 28465
(910) 278-5372

6. Paddle down the Davis Creek Canoe Trail. Bring a kayak or canoe (or rent one from Adventure Company in Southport), and paddle down the six-mile trail. Maps are available at the **Oak Island Recreation Center.**

Oak Island Recreation Center
3003 East Oak Island Drive
Oak Island, N.C. 28465
(910) 278-5518

EUE/SCREEN GEMS IN WILMINGTON

EASTERN N.C. | 131 miles south of Raleigh | **SCREENGEMSSTUDIOS.COM/NC**

I t's very clear, if you don't have a reason to be "on the lot" at EUE/Screen Gems Studios, you're not getting on the lot. Security guards in white shirts man the gatehouse, which is the only way in or out of the property.

About eight years ago, however, studio officials decided to open those gates to visitors each weekend.

"It's goodwill to the community," says Bill Vassar, executive vice president of EUE/Screen Gems. "The community is proud of the fact there's a studio here. It's locals who bring visitors from out of town to show them the studio."

Vassar's company is based in New York, where studios film shows including "Rachael Ray." But you have to go to Wilmington to walk in the same footsteps as stars such as Julia Roberts, Dennis Hopper, Dakota Fanning, and John Travolta.

On a tour, about 40 people gather with tickets in hand to see what gives Wilmington the nickname Hollywood East. Some even hope to catch a glimpse of a favorite TV star.

More than 500 feature films and television shows, like the TV drama "One Tree Hill," have filmed in Wilmington since 1984, and more business is expected since the state General Assembly recently approved a film incentives bill. At any one time, as many as five productions might be shooting on the lot.

BEHIND THE SCENES

Six guides — film or theater students from the University of North Carolina at Wilmington — take turns leading the group from the front of the property toward the massive nondescript metal warehouses called soundstages. As they rattle off the names of movies created here — *Divine Secrets of the Ya-Ya Sisterhood*, *Blue Velvet*, *Secret Life of Bees*, *Domestic Disturbance*, *Black Knight* — it's easy to imagine you're being led by the next great cinematographer or lead actress.

All 40 pairs of feet come to a halt as one guide stops in front of a small door leading into Sound Stage 7. She tells the group they are about to see a set for "One Tree Hill." A teenage girl wearing a "One Tree Hill" T-shirt beams.

It all started with *Firestarter* 26 years ago. Since then, EUE/Screen Gems Studios has been the site of more than 500 productions, including films, TV shows, and commercials.

VISIT
Screen Gems Studios
1223 23rd Street North
Wilmington, N.C. 28405

Public walking tours of
the studio are Saturday at
noon and 2 p.m. year-round.
From May to September
tours are Saturday and
Sunday at noon and 2
p.m. Reservations are not
required. Please arrive 15
minutes prior to tour time.
Admission is Adults $12,
students and military (with
valid ID) $10, seniors (65+)
$8, kids (5-12) $5, 4 and
younger are free.
(910) 343-3433

The door swings open to reveal what looks like a construction site, unfinished two-by-fours and electrical wiring. But just beyond appears to be the interior of a home. There's a living room with couches, books on the shelves, a kitchen with food in the cupboard, and even what looks like broccoli remnants in the sink.

The obvious difference is that this is all inside another huge building. And as massive as this soundstage seems, it's not nearly as cavernous as the newly built Stage 10, a 37,500-square-foot building, the largest soundstage in North America east of Los Angeles, California.

But even this smaller building, at 20,000 square feet, houses plenty of movie magic.

The guide explains that for water to come out of the sink, a garden hose is run to the faucet.

"Well, I had no idea all that was filmed here."

After each take, a special effects worker has to empty a bucket from a cabinet below the sink.

Visitors are free to peruse the "house" but are warned not to touch anything. Photos are not allowed throughout the tour because visitors are seeing sets that no one else has seen. Whole plots could be spoiled.

A toddler pulls at his mom's hand and says he wants to go upstairs.

"No, baby. It doesn't go anywhere. It just looks like it does. See?" she says, and points up to steps that go nowhere. The set for the second floor is at a separate part of the soundstage.

MAINTAINING THE ILLUSION

At Stage 5, the tour group learns that fans can keep film crews on their toes. The guide opens a refrigerator and pulls out a bottle of ketchup that expired in 2004 and a jar of peanut butter that expired in 2005. These props will never be eaten. But the guide says crew members are careful about rearranging the fridge every so often.

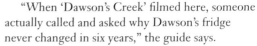

"When 'Dawson's Creek' filmed here, someone actually called and asked why Dawson's fridge never changed in six years," the guide says.

It does make you wonder how many other ways your favorite movies have fooled you.

A screening room is the last stop. Visitors are treated to a short film outlining some productions that called EUE/Screen Gems home. Iconic images of *Firestarter*, *Maximum Overdrive*, *Teenage Mutant Ninja Turtles*, *Muppets from Space*, and countless others flash across the screen.

And as the group is ushered back out of the gate under the watchful eyes of the security guards, an older man turns to his companion and says, "Well, I had no idea all that was filmed here."

— *Amy Hotz*

No reservations are required for the public Saturday tours that begin at the gatehouse at EUE/Screen Gems Studios. (No tours are given on the Saturdays following Christmas, Thanksgiving, Memorial Day, or Labor Day.)

For more than 200 years, the Dismal Swamp Canal has granted people access to the rich resources and breathtaking wilderness of the Great Dismal Swamp.

DISMAL SWAMP STATE PARK

EASTERN N.C. | 175 miles east of Raleigh | **NCPARKS.GOV**

B efore European explorers began to intrude in the 1700s, the Great Dismal Swamp stretched across more than one million acres, a rugged wilderness thick with forests, brush, and watery bogs.

As colonies bloomed along our nation's coast, however, it was only a matter of time before enterprising individuals would recognize the bounty hidden within the swamp's dark folds — mighty cypress and cedars waiting for souls hardy enough to harvest them. By 1793, construction was underway to build a canal that would connect the Chesapeake Bay to the Albemarle Sound.

In those early years, ambitious entrepreneurs, some led by George Washington, dreamed of taming the swamp. Attempts were made to drain it; the rich peat soil held such promise for farming. Nature, however, had other ideas, and a 160-year struggle ensued. In that time, timber operations succeeded in penetrating the forestland with canals and creeks; they floated millions of trees upstream to Norfolk, Viringia. But efforts to cultivate arable land failed. By the 1950s, with the last of the virgin forests cut, corporations withdrew, conceding that manmade tools were no match for the land's natural tendency to cover itself with water and shut out civilization.

Today, the Great Dismal Swamp is primarily a 107,000-acre national wildlife refuge that reaches across the North Carolina border into Virginia. Within that refuge, North Carolina has carved out a roughly 14,500-acre state park. Although it's now only a vestige of the natural wonder that Washington described as a "glorious paradise," the swamp still lures people with its beauty and mystery.

Far down the trail,

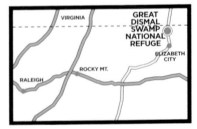

something moves. Signa Williams brings the binoculars up to her eyes. "Was that an otter?"

Turns out it was a bobcat, a little one. Not a baby, but born this year.

"Awesome," Williams breathes and resumes walking.

Williams is at work. She's a park ranger at the Dismal Swamp State Park. She loves her job.

As often as possible, Williams is out here, in this park that she knows intimately. She's been here since 2005, three years before the park opened to the public. Until 2008, only the hardiest of hikers crept into these woods.

The Great Dismal Swamp is one of the last wild places, not just in North Carolina, but on the East Coast. Even as a part of the state park system, this place is as untamed as it sounds. Visitors can't drive up to the park's center; they have to cross the Dismal Swamp Canal on a swing bridge, either on foot or a bike. Once they venture beyond the visitor center and a 900-foot boardwalk that allows easy access to the edge of the swamp, neatly managed amenities end.

And the majesty begins.

Whether covering the park's trails on foot or patrolling the dirt roads in her Ford Ranger, Williams doesn't rush. The park is 14,433 acres of forest wetlands, so thick in some places that sunlight barely reaches the ground. Nearly 18 miles of

State Park Ranger Signa Williams never tires of hikes through the Dismal Swamp, a setting rich with fresh sights, sounds, and experiences every day.

leftover logging trails give glimpses of the park's interior. Protected alongside the Great Dismal Swamp National Wildlife Refuge since the mid-1970s, this land is rich in wildlife and vegetation. Deer, turkeys, raccoons, otters, foxes, bobcats, and black bears wander these woods freely. This is not a place for speed.

As Williams makes her way down an old logging road, the vehicle occasionally lurching over ruts, she steps on the brake and hops out. She squats down on the trail and peers closely at a dark pile.

"I like to look down and see the stories the trail tells," Williams says.

This one is telling her a bear may be nearby. The pile is scat. And it's fresh.

The lead interpretation and education ranger, Williams is a natural storyteller. Every step in this rugged world triggers another story, another lesson.

She passes a coast pepperbush and runs her hand over a branch, stirring up a fragrance. "Smell the leaves," she says. "You don't think of a swamp as smelling pretty, but it does."

The trail winds its way through grape vines, blackberries, and cherry trees. A sign reading "No Bikes" is marred with jagged tooth marks. Williams tells of the mother bear who climbs the cherry trees, strips the branches, and hands them down to her cubs. Don't bother reaching up for a few for yourself, Williams says; they taste like cough syrup.

At the South Mills lock, the Pasquotank River rises to meet the Dismal Swamp Canal.

At the edge of the park, acres of haggard trees stand testimony to a massive fire that swept through the adjacent wildlife refuge in the summer of 2008. A light fire is good for the swamp, Williams explains, because it clears out the mature trees. But when fire burns down to the peat, it alters the soil's composition and thwarts some native species.

Walking the swamp, which is not as wet as you would imagine as it transitions largely to forest, Williams points out that the Great Dismal Swamp that George Washington tried to tame 200 years ago was full of cypress, gum, and Atlantic white cedar. Today, red maple, tulip poplar, and sycamore fill out the park.

"What's left is the heart of the swamp, the part that wouldn't give up," Williams says. "We can't restore the swamp to the pre-Colonial era. What we can do is take care of it, protect it, manage it."

'PAY ATTENTION' KIND OF PLACE

Williams knows some people are afraid of the swamp. They hear the word, and images of humid, dreary bogs crawling with threatening creatures come to mind.

That's not the Dismal. Trails here wind among massive hardwoods and flowering shrubs. Songbirds call to one another, hidden in the cover of dense brush. Deer, often as curious as the people who spot them, linger along the paths.

Williams does what she can to ease people's fears, to reassure them that here they are safe. "The swamp is not going to reach out and grab them," she says.

Be smart — stick to the trails, get back to the bridge before the park closes, don't approach any animals — and a day in the Dismal will be a journey unlike any other. You just have to slow down long enough to appreciate the swamp's raw beauty.

"It's a 'pay attention' kind of place," Williams says. "Take a little time to look at it, to breathe it … to listen to it. The swamp whispers — it doesn't shout."

— *Karen Haywood Queen*

The Dismal Swamp Canal still flows between Virginia's bay and North Carolina's sound, offering boaters a transformative path into a beautiful wilderness.

HOW TO EXPERIENCE THE DISMAL SWAMP:

1. Start with a visit to the welcome center, the only visitor center in the country where you can arrive by car or boat. Friendly staffers are happy to help you plan your Dismal Swamp adventure.

Dismal Swamp Canal Welcome Center
2356 U.S. Highway 17 North
South Mills, N.C. 27976
(877) 771-8333

2. And see it all by foot. Hike miles of winding trails — the original logging trails timbered by Moses White in the 18th century. And don't leave without getting a peek at the water with a stroll down the boardwalk. Tip: Pack binoculars to spot bobcats and white-tailed deer.

3. See it by water. See the swamp up close, and explore its waters via canoe or kayak.

4. See it by bike. Bring your own or borrow one from the welcome center, and peddle the three-mile, paved biking trail.

5. Pack a lunch. Enjoy an alfresco lunch at one of the many picnic tables beneath the shadow of towering pines. We recommend a pre-lunch stop at Belcrosse Bake Shoppe for sweet potato biscuits.

6. Cast a line into Lake Drummond, and catch any one of 23 different species of fish.

Dismal Swamp State Park
2294 U.S. Highway 17
South Mills, N.C. 27976
(252) 771-6593

7. Make a night of it. Set up camp — tent or RV — at **North River Campground and RV Park**. An onsite store has camping essentials, including marshmallows for s'mores. And the restaurant next door offers pizza, barbecue, and ice cream. Tip: Pick a spot on the lawn behind the lodge and wait for sunset to watch movies on the outdoor screen.

North River Campground and RV Park
256 Garrington Island Road
Shawboro, N.C. 27973
(252) 336-4414
NorthRiverCampground.com

N.C. Highway 12 shifts roles as it runs across the Outer Banks: A path through Hatteras Island's wilderness expanse and a link to coastal traditions in Cedar Island.

20 N.C. HIGHWAY 12 — BEACH ROAD

EASTERN N.C. | 175 miles east of Raleigh

The 148-mile, two-lane road that traverses the entire Outer Banks — N.C. Highway 12 — runs up the state's northern barrier islands like a spine, skirting along ocean, dunes, sound, and marsh, linking towns and communities and people, while providing access to the islands' four lighthouses, nearly a dozen museums, and thousands of places to sleep, shop, eat, and play.

To Outer Bankers, the road is more than pavement and paint, more than a means to an end. It is the iconic road to freedom. The path to reclining beach chairs, coconut-scented sunscreen, and crab cake dinners. The uncomplicated straight shot to the best surf breaks, the secret fishing holes, the duck blinds and boat ramps, the secluded beaches and wide-open spaces that put us at ease.

CEDAR ISLAND TO OCRACOKE

On the often overlooked southern end of the beach road is Cedar Island. It has only one store, Island's Choice Variety Store. Sherman Goodwin owns it. "There ain't a whole lot on our end of N.C. 12," he says.

But then the homegrown store owner proceeds to list all there is to do on his native Cedar Island: horseback riding, a campground on the beach, a restaurant and a motel, fishing, sound-side beaches, four boat ramps, hiking, and kayaking in the Cedar Island refuge. This is a remote place untouched by commercialism, as authentic a Down East experience as you're going to get.

It's quiet, except for a small surge of traffic when the Cedar

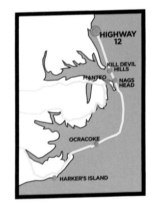

Island-Ocracoke Island ferry loads and unloads three times a day. Cars line up to wait for the ferry on the dead end of the road, and the Pamlico Sound stretches out beyond. The ride to Ocracoke Island is 23 miles, two hours and 15 minutes long, and the ferry spills its passengers out onto N.C. 12 in the heart of Ocracoke village.

OCRACOKE TO HATTERAS

In Ocracoke village, N.C. 12 is a road that almost requires you to walk or bike to get the full experience. It feels more like a lane than a highway.

Past the village, N.C. 12 begins its long foray through the Cape Hatteras National Seashore. Here, one can experience the Outer Banks in an almost-natural state. (The oceanfront dunes along the Outer Banks were manmade in the 1930s.) On the east side of the road are dunes and windblown scrub and the ocean beyond. On the west are maritime forest, marsh, and the Pamlico Sound.

The ocean is always near, and the National Park Service offers many opportunities for getting to it with ease.

Only 16 miles long on Ocracoke Island, N.C. 12 again is broken up

The Dare County Association of Fire Officers sells "South 12" stickers, appealing to locals who appreciate the road's significance, like Debbie Bell, co-owner of Rodanthe Surf Shop (opposite, on right).
Below: Travelers on N.C. 12 north of Rodanthe cruise through Pea Island National Wildlife Refuge, a popular destination for birders.

by a waterway and a ferry ride. But the Hatteras-Ocracoke Ferry is such a commonplace conveyance for getting to and from Ocracoke, it feels like it's part of N.C. 12. The 45-minute ferry experience is one of the last free rides left in life.

HATTERAS TO RODANTHE

On Hatteras Island, N.C. 12 travels 50 miles through seven small villages (Hatteras Village, Frisco, Buxton, Avon, Salvo, Waves, and Rodanthe) and through vast stretches of undeveloped Cape Hatteras National Seashore and Pea Island National Wildlife Refuge, with plenty of wildlife and birds to see. It's also where the road shows us just how uncomfortably narrow these barrier islands are in some places and how a highway built on a bed of sand is always at risk.

Before the paved roads on the Outer Banks, people drove on sand. They drove on the "inside road" down the center of the island, following in the tire ruts that were made before them. On nicer days, they "rode the wash" along the beach near the surf, bobbling along over sand hills and trying to avoid rushes of tide. Only the hardiest visitors braved these conditions.

When Outer Bankers came to the conclusion that they had to attract tourists to survive, they started building roads. The first paved road on the Outer Banks was in the Nags Head area in the 1930s. The roads on Hatteras and Ocracoke were paved in the 1950s, and the road to Corolla wasn't paved until the 1980s. The pavement smoothed over the ruggedness of the Outer Banks, but it also helped bring in all the comforts and conveniences and visitors the islanders now depend on.

TO COROLLA

In Kitty Hawk, you get some nice glimpses of the ocean, and then N.C. 12 veers up to the northern beaches — to Southern Shores, Duck, and the Currituck Outer Banks — and takes on the important role once again as a lifeline, the only road in or out. On the north end, N.C. 12 is set back farther from the ocean and rarely washes out.

Live oaks line the road, allowing just the occasional glimpse of Currituck Sound. The thriving village of Duck pops up on the landscape, the Sanderling makes an appearance, and then with a few dramatic twists and turns, you're in Currituck County, the last stretch of N.C. 12. The road here has only been paved for 25 years.

Cruising along north of Corolla Village, N.C. 12 ends at the edge of nowhere. The paved road gets sandy and then sandier. So you keep going, heading up along the beach toward Swan Beach and Carova, hoping to catch a glimpse of the area's wild horses, trying to imagine the Outer Banks before pavement.

— *Molly Harrison*

HOW TO EXPERIENCE THE BEACH ROAD:

1. Stop by the Ocracoke Lighthouse. Built in 1823, it's recognized as the oldest in the state and the second-oldest in the nation.

Ocracoke Lighthouse
360 Lighthouse Road
Ocracoke, N.C. 28465
(888) 493-3826

2. Horse around, and see the island's wild ponies at **Ocracoke Ponies and Pen**, a 180-acre pasture that's home to 24 equines.

Ocracoke Ponies and Pen
7669 Irvin Garrish Highway
Ocracoke, N.C. 28465
(888) 493-3826

3. Spy waterfowl at **Cedar Island National Wildlife Refuge**, where cooler months bring thousands of waterfowl from sea ducks to osprey.

Cedar Island National Wildlife Refuge
Lola Road at N.C. Highway 12
Cedar Island, N.C. 28520
(252) 926-4021

4. Hit more than 75 miles of protected beach at **Cape Hatteras National Seashore**. Chase crabs, build sandcastles, and even camp out (for a $20 fee). You can even climb all 248 spiral steps — equal to a 12-story building — to the top of the Hatteras Lighthouse.

Working at the ferry ticket booth in Cedar Island, Cindy Hanling (opposite) sees first-hand the importance of N.C. Highway 12.